FOSTERING CONNECTION

How Foster Families Can Tackle the Tough
Stuff and Raise Loving, Resilient Kids

Frank Grijalva, MSPH, MSCC

Fostering Connection: How Foster Families Can Tackle the Tough Stuff and Raise Loving, Resilient Kids

Copyright ©2025 Frank Grijalva.

Paperback ISBN: 978-1-967587-74-2
eBook ISBN: 978-1-967587-75-9

This publication is designed to provide accurate and authoritative information regarding the subject matter covered. It is sold with the understanding that the publisher is not engaged in rendering legal, accounting, or other professional services. If you require legal advice or other expert assistance, you should seek the services of a competent professional.

Design and cover art by Peaceful Profits.

Disclaimer: The author makes no guarantees to the results you'll achieve by reading this book. All business requires risk and hard work. The results and client case studies presented in this book represent results achieved working directly with the author. Your results may vary when undertaking any new business venture or marketing strategy.

TABLE OF CONTENTS

Love Them Anyway

Because you're reading this book, I'm assuming that you're a foster parent (or maybe you want to become one). That means you're doing one of the hardest, most beautiful things a person can do. You've opened your home to a child who's carrying a suitcase full of pain from neglect, abuse, or being bounced from one place to another like a ping-pong ball. You want to give these kids a safe place to land, a chance to heal, and maybe even a glimpse of what love feels like.

But let's be real: Some days it's overwhelming. The tantrums, the defiance, the moments when you catch them hiding food or shutting you out—they hit you like a freight train. You're left wondering, "Why do they act like this? Am I doing this wrong? Can I even handle this?"

I see you. I've been there. Not as a foster parent, but as one of those kids, scared and scrambled, trying to survive in a world that felt like it was out to get me.

I was born in Vallejo, California, 68 years ago to a 16-year-old mother who couldn't keep me or my younger brother. The state took us, citing neglect and abandonment, but mostly, it was the fact that she was young and unmarried in the 1950s.

The State of California placed us with adoptive parents who wanted to raise us to become priests in the Catholic Church. At first glance, that may sound like it would be a pleasant, quiet, and loving home. Unfortunately, it was anything but that. Their home wasn't a haven; it was a storm of physical and emotional abuse. My earliest memory is of my brother and me "decorating" the white leather seats of my adoptive daddy's brand new lemon-yellow Cadillac with a cigarette lighter, igniting a lifetime of fear.

That was my start, but it's not my story's end.

Recently, I drove back to Vallejo, now a trauma coach, to train foster care workers at a wonderful local program, called VOICES, which serves kids aging out of foster care. As I hit the city limits, Kelly Clarkson's "One Moment in Time" was playing on the radio. I teared up, overwhelmed by the weight of returning to my birthplace to help kids like me. That full-circle moment fuels this book.

Removed from a mom whose greatest flaw was that she was too young and too unmarried for the late 1950s, both of my new parents had grown up in challenging, abusive environments. When it came time to raise their own children, they simply repeated those same behaviors. It was what they knew.

I wasn't a "bad" kid, but their reaction to my energy was a reflexive attempt to control, suppress, and punish. And so began an abusive relationship. My brain was being wired through fear, always on high alert, awaiting the next blow.

Trauma and high stress do that to a kid. It wires your brain to be impulsive and reactive. It makes you see threats, even where there aren't any. Your brain feels like it's in permanent survival mode, constantly looking for opportunities to fight, flee, or freeze, just to get through the day.

My adoptive parents didn't understand that they were passing on their own trauma to me and my brother. They reacted to our normal kid behaviors with anger, punishment, and attempts to control us. Spoiler: That only made things worse. But I got through it. I found a way to heal and to forgive.

And I've spent the last 30 years helping others do the same. That's why I'm here—to give you the tools I wish my parents had, so you can love these kids through their chaos, equipping them to come out stronger on the other side.

This book isn't a textbook. It's not for therapists or PhDs. It's for *you*, the foster parent who's in the trenches, trying to figure out how to respond when a kid screams for no reason or hides under the bed when it's time for school.

You don't need a psychology degree to make a difference. What you need is curiosity, patience, and what I call *unconditional regard*—a way of looking at a child and saying, "I see you, not just your behavior, and I'm here for you, no matter what."

That's the heart of this book: Helping you understand some of the reasons why foster kids act the way they do and giving you practical, trauma-informed ways to respond that build trust, not walls.

Foster parenting is stepping into a kid's chaos heart first, determined to be their anchor. You've opened your home to a child carrying fear, loss, or pain. And they act out those emotions in unexpected ways. Maybe they hoard food, shut down, or push you away. Difficult moments can make you feel like you're failing, but you're not.

That kid isn't broken; they're surviving. Their brain has been wired by trauma and toxic stress. The ACEs (Adverse Childhood Experiences) study, which we will discuss in more detail later, shows that neglect, chaos, or abuse can shape a child's mind.

Their behaviors—screaming, hiding, lying—aren't (merely) defiance; they're instinctive survival strategies, like fight, flight, or freeze. This book is for you, foster parents, doing the hard, holy work of mentoring kids toward healing. You don't need to be perfect. You just need to show up, love them anyway, and keep going.

My personal story is not the worst by far, but it mirrors that of so many children you've probably already cared for. Taken from a young single mom when I was just 2 years old, my younger brother and I faced an adoptive home where my new father had PTSD from the Korean War and alcoholism, and my adoptive mother's mental health struggles, rooted in her own childhood of poverty and abuse. By age 14, I'd been to ten schools, struggling to fit in with each new group of neighborhood kids.

I didn't understand back then why I behaved the way I did. It took me almost 40 years of acting out, struggling, and dealing with the lasting consequences of my early trauma, until I saw myself reflected in the innocent faces of my own small children. That awakening prompted me to study, research, and eventually learn to heal. And now, over the second half of my life, I've learned through working with native tribes like the Tulalip and fostering families across the US. I've studied under clinicians, shamans, and even dolphins in the Navy.

I've seen what happens when we get this right: Kids begin to trust, parents feel empowered, and communities provide help and healing. You're here to lead with your heart, to mentor, and give back to kids who've faced fear and loss. Your job is to be their safe haven, showing them that there are people they can trust, one steady moment at a time.

This work is heavy. It'll test your heart and fill you with grief when things go wrong. As Maya Angelou said, "We did what we knew; when we knew better, we did better." Forgive yourself. You're learning, and you're enough. Love them anyway, but love yourself too.

Your strength is their foundation. The foster system is stretched thin. Resources and funding for important interventions can vanish overnight. Training is spotty, and you're often left to figure it out alone. This book gives you tools to be the coach these kids need: practical ways to stay calm, build trust, and protect your heart. Each chapter blends my story with science and offers you steps to navigate trauma's challenges, from food insecurity to running away. You'll learn to be a scientist, curious about their world, and a mentor, walking alongside them. I'm here for you too.

Here's how this book works. It's your user's manual, a guide you can pick up when a new kid comes into your care or when an old challenge pops up again. We've got 13 chapters, each tackling a common issue foster parents face like food hoarding, meltdowns, lying, or trouble at school. Each chapter follows the same rhythm:

- **A Story**: A real-life moment, either from my own childhood or my decades training foster care agencies, to show you what it's like for a kid in survival mode.
- **The Science**: A clear, no-jargon explanation of what's happening in the child's brain and body, translated so you can understand it without a science degree.
- **How to Respond**: Practical steps to handle the behavior in a way that heals, not harms, with examples for kids from toddlers to teenagers.
- **Practical Tools**: Exercises, reflections, and strategies to help you coach the child and protect your own emotional energy.

This isn't about quick fixes. Trauma can be deep and complicated, and it takes time to carve a new path. But every time you respond with patience, every time you choose connection over control, you're helping that child's brain learn what safety feels like. You're also protecting your own heart because fostering is a marathon, not a sprint, and your emotional battery needs to be replenished so you can persevere.

When I speak to groups of foster families, I talk a lot about "go zones" and "no-go zones." The go zone is where you stay curious, where you ask, "What happened to you?" instead of "What's wrong with you?" The no-go zone is where you react with anger, punishment, or you're worried about things you can't control. Like whether a kid will be moved tomorrow or what their future holds. Those no-go zones drain you, and they don't help the kid. This book will help you stay in the go zone, where healing happens.

I've spent 30 years working with trauma and toxic stress—collaborating with and being mentored by fantastic pioneers in trauma and brain science. I worked with esteemed, yet edgy, clinicians, Indigenous, foster care agencies, police officers, many children in the system, and even corporate CEOs (former foster youth like me). I've seen what happens when we get this right: Kids start to trust, parents feel empowered, and communities come together to support these kids.

This is the reason most of us began working with foster youth—to provide a safe environment so that a child will dare to grow, to serve, to lead with their heart, to mentor the next generation, and to give back. And it's why I'm inviting you to connect with me at the end of this book. I speak to foster family support groups, agencies, and anyone who wants to build a trauma-informed network for kids. If you're part of a group, reach out so we can keep this conversation going.

One more thing before we dive in: Fostering is unpredictable. A kid might be with you for a week, a year, or until they age out. You can't control that, and as much as we can get caught up in it, worrying about it is a no-go zone. What you *can* do is make every day count. Every time you show a kid they're worth loving, you're adding power to their prosocial resilience. You're giving them a tool they'll carry wherever they go whether it's brushing their teeth, trusting a teacher, or believing they're enough. That's your power as a foster parent. You don't have to be perfect. You just have to show up, love them anyway, and keep going.

All of which requires that you love yourself too. You've heard the phrase "hurting people hurt people"? Well, healed people help others heal too. We're going to spend a fair amount of time throughout this book ensuring that *you* are using your healing rituals, so that you are nurtured, healthy, and resilient, and you are adequately equipped to help the children in your care attain those same aspirations.

So, here's my ask: Commit to this journey with an open heart. Read this book one chapter at a time, try the tools, and lean on the resources you'll find in the appendix, like the National Child Traumatic Stress Network (NCTSN). You're not alone, and you're already doing something incredible.

Let me show you, in the pages of this book, exactly how to care for your children while also caring for yourself—without allowing the Department of Children's Services to control your life or your household.

Sincerely,
Frank Grijalva

Ready to talk about how I can help you navigate your challenges? Let's hop on a call at midwesttrauma.org

A QUICK WORD ABOUT MENTORS

I always thought I was built to do things myself. And I was intelligent and adaptive enough to survive, but it wasn't until I found a safe mentor that I began my healing journey and a holistic understanding of trauma. Dr. Robert Macy created sustained unconditional regard for me that allowed me to stretch and develop my curiosity.

Find your mentors; don't do it alone. In the Navy diver community, we learn that "2 is 1, 1 is none". And hopefully this book is the beginning of that for you.

Seeing the Storm– Understanding Trauma's Hidden Grip

CHAPTER 1

The Fear–Built Brain– Understanding Trauma and Survival Responses

As I mentioned, my earliest memory is a blur of fear in a lemon-yellow Cadillac with its white leather seats gleaming. I was maybe 3, left alone with my little brother in our adoptive parents' new car. They were smokers, so we knew how the cigarette lighter worked. On this sunny morning, we had been left alone to wait in the car while our parents ran an errand. Without their presence, we experimented. We discovered that the lighter made a distinctive circular black hole in the bright white leather seats. Delighted, we decided to "decorate" those seats with polka dotted burn marks. I remember feeling earnest and industrious. Until my parents returned.

My father, scarred by Korean War PTSD and alcoholism, and my mother, haunted by poverty and abuse, didn't see kids playing. They saw willful destruction. My father's harsh punishment left a perfect circular burn mark on my thigh that lingered for decades. My brother still carries a bald spot on the back of his head where the lighter struck him, even though more than fifty years have passed.

What does a 2- or 3-year-old child learn from searing intense pain delivered by an adult who is in a rage? They may learn to never do that again, but at what cost? Trust is lost, fear prevails, and the brain is wired to watch others in fear. On guard but with no understanding and no mentoring on how to return to safety in this relationship, a kid's brain isn't being taught how to trust or connect.

Our home was one where terror ruled. My father once chased 5-year-old me as I ran from him. When he realized he wasn't going to catch me, he threw a rock, knocking me down instead. My brain was built in fear, and I'm not alone.

I share my story to show how fear shaped my brain from the start. Foster youth in your home carry similar invisible scars, wired by trauma or toxic stress to survive, not thrive. Their yelling, hiding, or lying isn't about you; it's their brain's desperate bid to stay safe in a world that has felt anything but. As a foster parent, you're not just providing a bed—you're stepping into their storm, mentoring them toward trust. To do that, you need to understand what trauma is and how it builds a fear-based brain.

Let's unpack the science and survival strategies behind their behaviors so you can see their world more clearly and guide them with curiosity instead of control.

WHAT IS TRAUMA?

Trauma and toxic stress wire a child's brain differently, priming it for survival, rather than the connection that babies born into a "good enough" home are wired for.[1] Trauma can strike as a single event, like a car accident or witnessing violence. Or it can unfold as complex trauma, a relentless drip of neglect, abandonment, physical or emotional abuse across developmental phases and yes, even in the womb.[2]

My story began with the latter. That home, steeped in my adoptive father's alcohol-fueled PTSD and my mother's mental health struggles from her own abusive childhood, was a crucible of fear. Meeting my birth family in my 30s, and hearing the stories of my mom and her sisters' lives, has helped me understand that some genetic and environmental contributions affected my brother and me from the beginning as well.

Toxic stress is different from trauma, but they are interconnected. Toxic stress often looks like the grinding, unescapable chaos of poverty, home or food instability, or unpredictable caregivers, all of which combine to reshape a child's brain.[3] Much like the same way that water can carve deep trenches in the hardest of rock formations over time.

---

1   Bruce D. Perry and Maia Szalavitz (2006). *The Boy Who Was Raised as a Dog: And Other Stories from a Child Psychiatrist's Notebook—What Traumatized Children Can Teach Us About Loss, Love, and Healing.* (New York, Basic Books), 52.

2   Bessel A. van der Kolk, *The Body Keeps the Score: Brain, Mind, and Body in the Healing of Trauma* (New York: Viking, 2014), 97.

3   Jack P. Shonkoff et al., "The Lifelong Effects of Early Childhood Adversity and Toxic Stress," *Daedalus* 140, no. 2 (2011): 79–95, https://doi.org/10.1162/DAED_a_00045.

Imagine bringing home a healthy, beautiful plant from the nursery. If you then neglect it, not giving it the right amount of sun or water, it will begin to shrivel up and die. With the right food and sunlight, it begins to blossom within the household. If you have a neglected plant that you want to make healthy once again, then you need to understand that the more it has been neglected, the more care is required for recovery. You can't yell at it, isolate it, or punish it into recovery.

Foster kids arrive with their brain's alarm system, the amygdala and other structures, locked in overdrive, constantly scanning for danger.[4] Meanwhile, other vital parts of the brain—those responsible for logic, impulse control, and planning—remain underdeveloped because they aren't activated in the face of chronic toxic stress.

We'll talk more about this throughout the book, but basically it's like when your phone battery is getting low and it automatically switches to "low-power mode," which means that many nonessential systems are turned off to conserve battery power for those tasks which are more necessary. Those nonessential systems are eventually turned back on as soon as you've had time to plug your battery in and recharge.

Unfortunately, in our brains, those "nonessential" systems don't always have the luxury of being turned on because they can only turn on the whole brain in safety. Many of our children have not been in a safe, stable environment long enough for

---

4 Bessel A. van der Kolk, *The Body Keeps the Score: Brain, Mind, and Body in the Healing of Trauma* (New York: Viking, 2014), 97.

their brains to recognize that they are safe and can begin to turn on these other systems.[5]

One of the most accepted definitions of being traumatized is to experience an event, or multiple events, in which the child perceives that they or someone they love could die, that it's out of their control, and they can't escape it.[6] It is their *perception* that matters, not the reality of the events. We often dismiss injuries or events that the child has experienced and internalized because we can see the bigger picture of the situation. We see their behavior but because there are no visible wounds, we can too often dismiss these behaviors as children being naughty rather than the effects of trauma in a developing brain.

This can be the beginning of a confusing emotional and behavioral avalanche for everyone.

This isn't "bad behavior"; it's survival. Their brain defaults to strategies honed in fear: fight (yelling, hitting), flight (running, hiding), or freeze (shutting down, dissociating), often referred to as an "involuntary threat response."[7] As a foster parent, your role isn't to judge these responses, but rather to mentor kids through them, guiding them toward trust and safety with patience and curiosity. Sometimes we have to get reactive when there is a chance of someone getting hurt. Debriefing, knowing

---

5　Bruce D. Perry and Maia Szalavitz, *The Boy Who Was Raised as a Dog: And Other Stories from a Child Psychiatrist's Notebook—What Traumatized Children Can Teach Us About Loss, Love, and Healing* (New York: Basic Books, 2006), 47.

6　Bessel A. van der Kolk, *The Body Keeps the Score: Brain, Mind, and Body in the Healing of Trauma* (New York: Viking, 2014), 56.

7　Ibid, 97.

how the brain works, and creating and practicing a proactive plan afterward is critical.

WHAT YOU SEE

Foster kids experience trauma two to two-and-a-half times more than kids from "good enough homes."[8] How they get there is the result of millions of examples of not knowing better, impulse, and finding out the hard way.

At 9, my family was living in Panama's Canal Zone. One day, I stepped on glass while playing outside barefoot, despite my adoptive parents' oft repeated rules to always wear shoes. The gash bled profusely, but I didn't cry. And I definitely didn't tell them. Terrified of their anger more than the physical pain, I wrapped my foot in a dirty towel and hid the injury for days, limping through school. When my parents did finally discover my injury and took me to the doctor, they were shocked to learn how close I had been to losing my foot completely due to infection. The doctor said, "If you had brought him in 12 hours later, we would be taking his foot."

That decision to hide my injured foot wasn't rooted in stubbornness; it was survival. My fear-built brain was prioritizing avoidance of my parents' anger over my own desire to walk pain-free. I couldn't trust them to take care of me. Fear was in control because I had no reason to expect that my parents would respond in any way other than how my father had reacted when I "decorated" his new car. Nothing was ever

---

8 "Improving Services for Children, Youth, and Families," OVC 2017 Report to the Nation, Office for Victims of Crime, June 2017, https://ovc.ojp.gov/sites/g/files/xyckuh226/files/pubs/reporttonation2017/children-youth-families.html

done to change the way I had experienced that event. My brain assumed that every similar situation would garner the same response from my parents—anger, yelling, and (often) physical punishment.

Without re-attunement, extensive consoling, and nurturing of the young child, there is no stimulation of those parts of the brain related to logic and future consequence. The brain is activated and fueled by the fear of remembered physical punishment.

Foster kids often act in unexpected ways; their brains are wired for survival. You might find food stashed under their bed because the memory of hungry nights continues to haunt them. Or you may catch them lying about small things, an instinctive response to dodge disapproval and shame. You can't always know what drives their behavior, so stay calm and curious. Frustration without clear communication and an established relationship is a no-go zone.

Meltdowns, like tantrums, screaming, and throwing objects, signal overwhelming emotions that are difficult to name. A blank stare or refusal to move might be their brain's response to an uncertain, chaotic environment.[9] These aren't acts of defiance; **they're involuntary.** They're tools of a brain wired to survive. It takes time to trust. The experience of the child is often that they are most hurt when they let their guard down. So they will use a lot of energy pushing against your boundaries, testing the safety of the home you provide for them. Their life depends on it.

---

9 Bessel A. van der Kolk, *The Body Keeps the Score: Brain, Mind, and Body in the Healing of Trauma* (New York: Viking, 2014, 97.

Let me share a quick pro tip I learned from my mentors Dr. Robert Macy and Dr. Sandra Bloom called **QTIP: Quit Taking It Personally!**

Practice it. Internalize it. Your emotional life will be so much better for it. Their reactions aren't about you. These behaviors are echoes of a past where safety was nonexistent. Stay curious instead of defensive. Ask yourself, "What's driving this?" instead of reacting harshly. Your calm presence signals that you're a safe haven rather than another threat. It's easy to dismiss behavior we don't understand. Remember: This child's threat detection system was likely built to react to subtle, micro-cues that you might not even be aware you are doing. For them, it can be the first sign of terror, triggering a violent reaction.

This "involuntary threat response" is something we all experience at some point in our emotional lives, and it's important to remember that it is a brain in survival.

THE SCIENCE: A FEAR-BASED BRAIN

Trauma shrinks a child's capacity to trust, keeping their amygdala (their "survival" brain, located at the base of a person's skull, just above the start of the spinal column) on high alert. This stunts the prefrontal cortex's growth (located at the front of your brain, in your forehead). Because of this, kids' brains are reactive, not reflective; their nervous system is primed for danger.[10] Bessel van der Kolk emphasizes that

10 Bruce D. Perry and Maia Szalavitz, *The Boy Who Was Raised as a Dog: And Other Stories from a Child Psychiatrist's Notebook—What Traumatized Children Can Teach Us about Loss, Love, and Healing* (New York: Basic Books, 2006).

this emergency threat detection system stays "on," scanning for threats even in safe settings, like your home.[11]

My adoptive home, with its volatile mix of parental responses to my youthful behaviors, kept me in this state. I was always braced for the next blow, like the rock my father threw to stop me from running away from him or my mother threatening me with a soup ladle while counting the number of times I chewed each bite of food. It probably won't be a surprise to you that I learned how to throw rocks as accurately as my dad, and I continue to struggle with food issues to some extent, thanks to my mom.

Nobel Laureate Daniel Kahneman's research on repetition offers a coaching framework, suggesting it takes approximately 11 exposures for a new experience to feel familiar, and familiarity makes it more likely to happen. Then it takes an additional 20 to 40 repetitions to begin to forge a new neural synapse. It's the brain responding to repeated activity that helps them begin to actually *trust* you won't shame them for mistakes.[12]

A foster kid's brain, built in fear, defaults to survival responses: fight, flight, or freeze. These behavior patterns kept them alive in chaotic or abusive environments in the past.[13] Toxic stress compounds this by elevating stress hormones, which

---

11 Bessel A. van der Kolk, *The Body Keeps the Score: Brain, Mind, and Body in the Healing of Trauma* (New York: Viking, 2014).

12 Daniel Kahneman, *Thinking, Fast and Slow* (New York: Farrar, Straus and Giroux, 2011).

13 Bruce D. Perry and Maia Szalavitz, *The Boy Who Was Raised as a Dog* (New York: Basic Books, 2006), 47.

can disrupt emotional regulation and memory formation. Additionally, once chaos becomes a habit, people young and old will often work to *maintain* chaos because that's the state that they are comfortable in, even though it is not necessarily safe.[14]

Yet, all is not lost. Consistent, caring relationships rewire these survival responses, gradually calming the amygdala and strengthening the prefrontal cortex.[15] Your steady presence and the guidance you provide your child with a new strategy brings the science to life, reshaping their brain one safe interaction at a time.

HOW TO RESPOND

Your job isn't to overhaul their brain. It's to be a safe haven, a steady anchor in their storm. When they lash out or hide, stay calm. If you can't (because we're only human, after all), recover as quickly as possible. Acknowledge your reaction, apologize, and tell your child why it's important for you to reconcile. Attempting to control or punish when you are angry or frustrated will only trigger more fear and damage the trust you have begun to build.[16]

Use curiosity: "What's going on for you?" or "What do you need right now?" shows that you're not the enemy. Consistency is your superpower—showing up daily and keeping promises builds trust.

---

14 Bessel A. van der Kolk, *The Body Keeps the Score* (New York: Viking, 2014), 89.

15 Daniel J. Siegel, *The Developing Mind* (New York: Guilford Press, 2012), 112.

16 Sarah Pemberton and Wendy Wheeler, *Trauma-Informed Parenting for Foster and Adoptive Families* (Independently published, 2023), 45.

QTIP keeps you grounded when their survival strategies feel personal. Act like a scientist: observe their triggers (e.g., loud voices that lead to sudden behavior changes), and tailor your approach. Avoid consequences that feel like control; instead, use calm talks to set boundaries, like, "What's the easiest way for me to know that you need a snack?"

Over the years, the most successful strategy has been abundance rather than restriction until safety and relationships are established. Without safety and relationship, their brains perceive you as something they have to work around, not someone they can trust. Mentor, don't manage. Your curiosity and consistency show them safety is real, rewiring their brain for connection.

PRACTICAL TOOLS

- **Curiosity questions**: Ask, "What do you need right now?" to show you're safe.
- **Consistency ritual**: Set a daily connection moment—bedtime chats, breakfast check-ins.
- **QTIP check**: When triggered, pause, breathe, and remind yourself: Quit Taking It Personally.
- **Safety antra**: Say things like, "You're safe with me," to calm their nervous system.
- **Observe like a scientist**: Note their triggers (e.g., loud voices) to tailor your approach.

MOVING FORWARD

Your foster kid's brain is wired for survival, but you're rewiring it for trust. Every calm moment and every curious question lays a brick in their wall of security and resilience. Next, we'll explore how to be their safe haven by turning fear into connection.

CHAPTER 2

Becoming a Safe Haven–Your Role in Building Trust

In my adoptive home, trust was nonexistent, creating an environment that could explode without warning. My understanding of the definition of "love" was a distorted minefield. One day, my mom would shout a harsh, shaming tirade for a minor misstep, and the next, a brutal inescapable beating. Every day, I lived between fear and tension. Because I grew up, from a very young age, physically overwhelmed by my parents' abuse and unable to defend myself, my nervous system was wired for flight. My brain was always seeking to be one step ahead of the next threat.

In the most terrifying of situations, dissociation would set in. My body would be present, but my mind would run as far away as possible. Those lessons carved deep grooves into my growing brain, teaching me that safety was a lie and trust was a risk I couldn't afford. In one particularly brutal beating, I remember watching myself from across the room at one point. When it was over and my parents discovered that I didn't do whatever it was that I was being punished for, my mother's response was "Well, you probably deserved it anyway."

What does a 12-year-old do with that?

Years later, as a trauma coach in a residential program, I met an 11-year-old girl whose eyes carried the same wariness I'd known. She'd been through multiple foster homes before arriving at this group home, her trust shattered by men who'd hurt her. During a group activity, I commented lightly on the actions of another student that she did not agree with. It was an innocent remark to me, but to her it was a trigger that echoed something from her past that I could never have known in advance. She quickly moved around the corner of the building to an area where a window had been broken recently. Sharp pieces of glass that had been missed in cleanup lay on the ground, partially covered by leaves and grass.

Her sudden shift in behavior made me curious. Following a few paces behind her, I found her crouched, one hand clutching jagged glass shards, her other hand trembling as she picked up another piece. Even though my gut instinct was to call her away from the danger, I sensed there was something deeper here that I needed to understand and honor.

What I saw was that she wasn't just playing with danger; she was cueing me, trying to force a confrontation with me. It was as if her survival brain was screaming, "Let's get this over with!"

I kneeled a safe distance away, keeping my voice soft and steady. "You're really looking out for everyone, keeping us safe by picking up all those pieces of glass," I said, nodding at the remaining pieces strewn on the ground. Her eyes flickered with surprise. She'd expected anger, a confrontation, a restraint, a trauma reenactment—not praise. I held out my hand, not demanding, but inviting. "Can I hold those for you? I'll keep them safe." Slowly, she handed me the shards, her shoulders easing as she saw I wouldn't lash out. She picked up the remaining shards and then we walked together back to the group.

That moment wasn't magic—it was unconditional regard, showing her that I saw her strength, not her "problem." I'd been that kid, hiding pain to survive, and I knew her fear. She wasn't going to trigger me into a controlled response.

The standard institutional approach when a kid is holding glass shards would be pressurized speech, looming over her, demanding she drop the shards. But those actions would only trigger a trauma reenactment, pulling her back into her history of immobilization and punishment. Her brain sought to force me to respond in a way that she was familiar with, even as she feared it, to match her warped perception of the world as unsafe and hostile. Instead, I stayed calm, recognizing this as her survival strategy, not defiance, and slowly, over time, she began to trust me.

Let me say that another way: The typical response could easily be to quickly grab her, force her hands open, remove the shards "before she is injured." In reality, that IS the injury—holding her immobilized, forcing her to obey an adult physically. So, her actions begin to trigger the very response she dreads. And we have to be paying attention to gently and calmly affect a change in situation or behavior without accidentally retraumatizing her through our own threat response. So in effect, she is training you to act like her abusers have in the form that she is most familiar with.

But don't get me wrong. There will certainly be times when you MUST step in physically. And then, you must rebuild trust and reestablish that safe connection as quickly as possible. It can be a delicate tightrope to navigate with any given child—do I step in or not? It helps to know your child well, but you don't always have the luxury of time with a child before their trauma response is triggered. You have to react as best as possible and then be prepared for "damage control" of your relationship afterward.

What I'm talking about here is the living out of this trauma-response model:

- Protect
- Re-attune
- Plan
- Practice

As I learned in the Navy Diver community, proper *prior* preparation prevents poor performance. Preparing your relationship for the possibility of needing to take "extreme measures," talking about it, and making and planning a different plan in advance can pave the way for a smoother transition back to a safe relationship after a negative situation occurs. When you help a kid learn a different way, beyond violence or trauma reenactment, they benefit—as does everyone they encounter in the future.

WHAT'S A SAFE HAVEN?

A safe haven is you—calm, consistent, curious—becoming the steady anchor a foster kid can rely on when their world feels like a storm. Trauma wires kids to expect danger at every turn, their brains primed to misread a raised eyebrow or sharp tone as a threat. Your presence, soft voice, neutral face, and predictable actions can rewrite the script, showing that trust is not just possible, but also real. This isn't about being perfect; it's about being present, day after day, proving you're not another source of chaos.

QTIP: Quit Taking It Personally. When a kid melts down, slams doors, or pulls away, it's not about you—it's their fear-built brain reacting to a past where safety was scarce. My adoptive home taught me trust was a trap, so it was better to remain on guard and expect pain. As a foster parent, you're reframing that conditioning and unconscious habit not by forcing connection, but by being a reliable haven. Shift your mindset so that you're not seeking to be their controller, demanding compliance, but rather become their mentor, offering a space where they can exhale and begin to believe in safety.

Imagine a kid who flinches when you reach over their shoulder because their body is braced for a blow. That's trauma's imprint, not defiance. Your job is to notice—like a scientist, curious about their cues, compassion activated—and respond with steadiness. A soft "I'm here when you're ready" or a quiet nod can signal you're different from the chaos they've known.

This work is subtle but powerful. Every time you stay calm, you're laying a brick in their path of trust, helping them see your home as a refuge, not a battlefield.

THE SCIENCE: CONNECTION HEALS

Science backs this up: Relationships are the engine of healing for traumatized kids. In the opening paragraph of the chapter on child abuse in Judith Lewis Herman's book, *Trauma and Recovery*, she writes:

> The child trapped in an abusive environment is faced with the formidable tasks of adaptation. They must find a way to preserve a sense of trust in people who are untrustworthy, safety in a situation that is unsafe, control in a situation that is terrifyingly unpredictable, power in a situation of helplessness. Unable to care for or protect themselves, they must compensate for the failures of adult care and protection with the only means at their disposal, an immature system of psychological defenses.[17]

We too often assume that because we are looking at a 15-year-old, they have all the tools that a 15-year-old should have. The reality is that they are showing us what they do have when they disintegrate under the stressors they are exposed to.

Think of a kid's nervous system as a frayed wire, sparking at every touch. Trauma keeps it live, ready to jolt at a loud voice or sudden move. Co-regulation is you slowly reducing the power to that wire; your calm presence reroutes the energy

---

17 Judith L. Herman, *Trauma and Recovery: The Aftermath of Violence—from Domestic Abuse to Political Terror*, 2nd ed. (New York: Basic Books, 2015), 96.

into healthier responses. Your consistency becomes the insulation that protects that wire from short-circuiting. This works because the brain is "plastic"—flexible and malleable, able to be reshaped, especially in kids. You may recognize the term "neuroplasticity." Each time you stay steady, you're helping their amygdala, the fear center, calm down, while their prefrontal cortex, the part that plans and trusts, grows stronger.

Not long ago, I was coaching a 13-year-old child who lied about earning a martial arts belt. He had spouted a quick lie to mask his fear and intimidation. His brain was trying to project mastery and power through his bold, obvious lie. Instead of calling him out, I commented with respect, "Wow, that must have been a lot of very hard work. Good for you!" By ignoring the details and not challenging the narrative, I bypassed his brain's expectations completely. I didn't care that he lied. It was unimportant to me. What was far more important was that he began to trust me. My curiosity built a bridge and, over several weeks, he started sharing truths, dropping the lies, discussing real events, his trust growing with each safe interaction. Your presence does the same, allowing the development of safety into trust, one moment at a time.

But building that bridge isn't always easy; it's messy, and you'll stumble. Their lies or tests can feel personal, pushing you to react fast or try to fix it all. I've been there, guessing wrong and learning the hard way that trust takes time and humility. That's where your steady presence shines, even when you don't have all the answers.

POSSIBLE WAYS TO RESPOND

Keep in mind that "guessing correctly" only comes with vast experience, and still only occurs SOME of the time, never *always*. You won't get it right every time. And, honestly, I *still* don't always get it right either, even after decades of working with foster youth.

Being a safe haven means staying unconditional, even when a kid pushes you away or tests your patience. They might yell, hide, or shut down not to hurt you, but to protect themselves. Don't chase control because it triggers their fear response. Instead, offer safety.

Years ago, I worked with a 15-year-old girl in a group home who'd slam her door at the start of every group meeting. Staff saw defiance; I saw fear. I started leaving her a note before meetings: "Join us when you're ready, no pressure." One day she showed up, silent but present. That was trust budding not because I forced her, but because I gave her the space to choose.

You can do this too. If a kid runs, don't pursue unless safety demands it. Offer a safe spot, like a cozy blanket in a quiet corner that they can return to. If they lash out, check your tone. A sharp "Stop it!" can echo the chaos of their past, while a soft "I'm here, let's figure this out" signals safety.

We often get caught up in the "It's a tough world out there, they have to learn." Unfortunately, this can lead to a self-fulfilling prophecy if you insist that the world out there is tough. That message, repeated over and over, creates conditioning in a child's brain, which then, in turn, creates their reality.

Life doesn't have to be tough. It can be loving, safe, and connecting. But they can't learn that if they aren't exposed to it. The problem is, they cannot learn from you until their brains are calm enough to listen, and that first requires the existence of a trusting relationship.

Mistakes happen. If you accidentally trigger them—a sigh, a frown—apologize quickly: "I'm sorry, that was my stress, not you." Repeatedly reminding them that they are not the reason you are reacting allows them to minimize their defensiveness and begin to put themselves in other people's shoes. This is part of the beginning of empathy.

This re-attunement, like rocking a baby back to calm, rebuilds trust. Be a scientist. Observe their cues. Does a loud laugh make them flinch? Does a quick move spark a freeze? Tailor your approach. I once coached a foster mom whose 10-year-old foster son froze at raised voices. We know from the science of the last 30 years that the ability to comprehend what is being said is likely compromised in that moment of frozen fear. Words don't matter. Tone and physical proximity become the most important ways to produce safety. She started speaking softly during tense moments, moving so her body didn't feel threatening, and over time, he began to relax. His nervous system began to sync with her calm.

A moment of re-attuning is often necessary. Re-attuning means an adult apologizes to an adolescent or teen for whatever the adult may have done or said, or failed to do or say, which triggered a negative response in the child. This moment of "I'm sorry that scared you", or "I apologize for rolling my eyes when you spoke. I am tired. It's not a reflection on how I feel about spending time with you." It removes the feelings of fear or shame from the child, and models reconciliation. A child can't learn to reconnect without repeated modeling of authentic reconciliation from adult mentors.

When you are working with a child to help them re-attune, avoid using the words "if" or "but" as much as possible. More on that later.

QTIP keeps you grounded. Their reactions are their trauma talking, not a judgment of you. Stay curious by asking, "What's going on for them?" to guide your response.

PRACTICAL TOOLS

Here are tools and practical steps to make you a safe haven and build trust without controlling:

- **QTIP check**: When a kid's meltdown spikes your frustration, pause, take a deep breath, and silently say, "Quit Taking It Personally." This resets your mindset, keeping you calm. Practice it daily—it's your anchor.
- **Apology to re-attunement**: If your tone or look triggers fear, say, "I'm sorry. That wasn't about you; I was just tired." This small act repairs trust, showing you're human but safe.
- **Safe space setup**: Give kids two retreat spots they can choose, like a beanbag in a quiet corner or a closet with pillows. Let them pick, honoring their need for control. A foster kid I coached claimed a hallway nook; it became his sanctuary.

- **Connection moments**: Build daily rituals, like a morning check-in ("How's your day starting?") or a bedtime chat ("What's one good thing today?"). These predictable moments signal safety. I have worked with many residential staff and foster parents who have set up a chair or space near the child's bedroom door so that their bedtime ritual, over time, became an opportunity to talk about the day.
- **Tone watch**: Keep your voice soft, your face open and gentle.

PROTECTING YOUR HEART

This work is heavy. Kids' pain can stir your own shame or exhaustion. You'll mess up. I did early in my coaching when my rushed tone sent a 9-year-old foster boy hiding under a table, thinking I was angry. I apologized, sat on the floor, and waited. He came out, and we rebuilt trust. Forgive yourself when you stumble; you're learning, just like the kids. Love yourself too. Rest when you're drained, breathe through stress, and seek support from friends or a counselor.

Think through the aspects that you are modeling during this moment of slow, deep breathing to calm yourself—focusing your attention, clearing your mind, and modeling what you want to see while also modeling the benefits of restoration and connection. Intentionally adjust your facial muscles, vocal tone, and shoulders—these are visible cues that kids will notice. Know what you are doing and how you are being perceived so that you can positively affect the outcome you desire and teach a new perspective.

You've probably already heard this about your visual cues 100 times, but have you ever heard WHY it's important? **You're modeling co-regulation to a young person who has never experienced it before.**

Your strength is their foundation, but you can't pour from an empty cup. I learned this while in the US Navy working with trained dolphins—yes, dolphins—whose trust required my patience and calm. If I was off, they sensed it. Same with kids. Protect your heart and you'll be the safe haven they need.

Next, we'll tackle food insecurity, a common trauma challenge.

CHAPTER 3

The Banana Incident–Food Insecurity and Control

As I've already said, my adoptive home wasn't a place of warmth or plenty. Food was a battleground—locked in cabinets, rationed like we were in a war zone. I'd often lie awake at night, stomach growling not just for food, but for something deeper, something I couldn't name. Safety, maybe. A promise that tomorrow wouldn't be as hard as today.

When we kids were lying in bed, overwhelmed, we were listening through the lens of fear to all the sounds in the house. Once it got quiet, a child subconsciously thinks of ways to "defeat the system," whether that's how to access the food or finding a sense of control.

It was not conscious rebellion but rather the underlying response to fear-based need. "The sense of accomplishment when you were holding the food in your hand," was how one boy described it. Whether hoarding or gorging, often the accomplishment came from knowing YOU were in control of the food. I still remember the first time I was able to buy a whole gallon of milk *just for myself*. The satisfaction is something that, at the age of 68, I still savor: control.

One day, when I was about 5 or so, I was monitoring the activity in the house. My mom had just returned from grocery shopping. On the counter, along with the government cheese and the powdered milk, was a beautiful, mouthwatering bunch of ripe bananas that caught my attention. I impulsively grabbed one from the bunch. As I heard its sharp snap of release, I wasn't thinking about survival. I was simply hungry.

Suddenly, my adoptive mom turned on me, her face like thunder, eyes blazing with something I'd later call betrayal. "You little thief," she spat. "You didn't ask permission." I froze, ripe fruit clinging to my lips, shame flooding my chest. Her punishment wasn't a lecture or a time-out. She grabbed the rest of the bananas from the counter—seven, eight, maybe ten—and slammed them in front of me.

"You want to eat? Fine. Eat them. All of them. *Now*." Surprisingly, I remember feeling pleased. *All of them?* Yes! I dug into my assigned task quite happily, which only increased her rage. I was doing what she asked me to do, and I liked it, which made her even angrier. I couldn't understand her rage, only confusion. At 5 years old, here was yet another situation where I couldn't trust what adults said. I was too young to understand the disconnect between her words and what she *meant*.

That moment stuck with me, though: the shame, the bewilderment, the fear, the belief that I'd never be safe. It shaped how I saw food, control, and even trust—for decades.

I'd hide snacks in my room, eat in secret, sneak into the kitchen at night, defeat locks, and locate the most obscure hiding spaces.

No connection was built between my parents and me. No sense of safety. Just a brain struggling to make sense of the world around me, fighting for some type of control, and always waiting for the other shoe to drop.

If you're a foster parent, you've probably seen this in your own home. Maybe it's a kid stuffing granola bars under their pillow, sneaking leftovers from the fridge, or eating until they're sick. Maybe they refuse to eat at the table, or they hoard food like it's their lifeline.

It's maddening, isn't it? You're trying to feed them and show them you are a safe person, but they're acting like you're the enemy. I'm here to tell you: It's not about you. It's about what trauma has done to their brain, their body, and their soul.

A 14-year-old girl in a residential treatment facility, with a history of foster care and violence, often clashed with staff due to her aggressive behavior. Her actions stemmed from food insecurity, worsened by staff bringing in fast food for themselves while she faced dietary restrictions. This sparked resentment against what she perceived as unfair treatment. This sense of "unfairness" is a common trigger for adolescents with traumatic backgrounds, especially for those who are sensitive to social justice issues.

Staff often focused on managing her aggression rather than addressing its root cause. The team was committed to implementing trauma-informed care. When I came in for a consultation, we discussed her food insecurity in a team meeting. Instead of punishing her behavior, we provided a large bowl of her favorite snacks—dried fruit, carbs, candy, and nuts—divided into single-serving baggies. Staff gave her one baggie hourly **regardless of behavior**. Although initially resistant, the staff followed through, and within three weeks, her aggression toward them stopped. After a few more weeks, she began saving baggies to enjoy during TV time. Later, she began holding some back to share with her peers.

This approach considered three factors: her history of food insecurity, which drove her emotions; the long-term duration of food insecurity; and its impact on her development phases across various ages and stages where she learned or failed to learn appropriate concepts of safety and security. For example, a 3-year-old perceives food insecurity differently than a 6-year-old, who perceives food insecurity differently than a 9-year-old.

And of course, by the time she was 14, all of these emotions and fears were jumbled together in the subconscious areas of her mind, along with the memories of prior punishment-based interventions.

By addressing the root cause—food insecurity—we interrupted the cycle of escalating behavior staff response known as "environmental conditioning," which would have labeled her as a dangerous criminal. This likely would have led to incarceration or worse.

At her adoption ceremony 18 months later, she ran up to thank me. She acknowledged the "food thing" helped her, and now she said she no longer needed it.

This shows the necessity of individualized solutions. Foster parents and social workers need better access to trauma-informed coaching support to learn how to create tailored strategies for children with trauma. This case highlights the importance of meeting a child's unique needs in a supportive environment, which should be the standard in foster care nationwide.

That's exactly why I wrote this book—to help you not only discover but actually **USE** these tools, so you can successfully help more children move from surviving to thriving.

THE SCIENCE

Let's talk about what's happening inside a kid like me when we sneak food. Trauma begins to rewire our brains when hunger or neglect or abuse is so intense that we perceive that we might not survive. Through those experiences, a child's brain is conditioned toward impulsiveness and reactivity. Their brain is reacting in the "immediacy of the moment."

While well-meaning, when adults try to control food access, it often triggers an involuntary threat response—the very behaviors you are trying to avoid! Ultimately, this also inhibits connection and trust-building—the things you *do* want.

Trauma—whether it's hunger, neglect, or abuse—rewires the brain to prioritize survival. Picture a light switch in the brain flipped to "on" and stuck there. That's the amygdala, the part that screams, "Danger! Protect yourself!" When a kid has gone hungry too often or lived for too long in chaos, the amygdala stays lit up, constantly scanning for threats. And when that happens, the brain becomes hyperaware of everything happening around the child.

Interestingly, though, it has no understanding of what's happening *inside* the child. What this means is that the child struggles to understand or recognize their own feelings. They are far more comfortable reacting to the feelings of other people around them.

Things are very black and white in that part of the brain. They develop a singular focus, even obsessive at times, about their access to what they think they need. Safety is the only thing that is going to give the brain a sense of calm and an ability to learn and grow into new levels of thinking.

Remember, this is the *kid's* perception of safety, not yours.

Food becomes a trigger because it's tied to their brains understanding of what they need to survive. Stealing, hoarding, and overeating are not about being bad or greedy. It's the brain saying, "This might be your last chance to eat. Grab some more."

Here's where it gets deeper: Studies looking at brain development over time suggest that trauma doesn't just mess with the amygdala. It *starves* the left hemisphere of oxygen and energy, where comprehension, verbalization, linear and logical thinking exist for most people. This, in turn, changes the prefrontal cortex, which is the brain's control center. That's the part that helps you think logically, plan ahead, and control impulses. When a kid's under chronic stress, the prefrontal cortex takes a backseat and the amygdala, the emotional center, drives the show.

So, when they're shoving food in their pockets or eating until they're sick, they're not plotting to annoy you. They are reacting like a cornered animal because their brain is stuck in survival mode.

I tell parents this all the time: When you're in that state, how many words do you know? Picture yourself in a screaming match with someone you love and you are so mad you can't think straight. How many words do you remember in the heat of the moment? You're down to a handful of the worst kind of words, right?

And it's not just your words that are changed. Your facial expression, your stance, your tone of voice—all of it is different. You didn't deliberately decide to look or act a particular way. It was automatic, an "involuntary threat response." That's what it's like for these kids, except it's not just one fight. It's their whole world.

Then there's another layer called *epigenetics*. This is how trauma affects the way a kid's genes work. If they've gone hungry for years, their body might "learn" to expect scarcity, like it's writing a survival manual in their DNA. Their metabolism, their stress response, and their focus on food all get tuned to "there's never enough." It's like their nervous system is a capacitor charged up with tension and ready to pop. That's why food becomes such a battleground. They're not fighting you— they're fighting a past that taught them trust is a trap.

I saw this in action while learning from a Native American tribe in Washington. Indigenous populations experience high levels of exposure to toxic stressors and trauma.[18] The adult reaction was that these children needed to learn to control themselves. This is true, however, the problem is that adults are starting from a point of rational thinking, while a child with no relationship with you is starting from a reactive, self-focused survival brain.

In working at one of the schools with a large percentage of Indigenous kids, I learned from the Native liaison who kept her room fully stocked with all types of snacks. As the children came to understand that the food was there for them, no matter what, they began to take less food. But they would continue to stop by, say hi, and glance at the food before heading to class. There was no fight; they knew food was consistently available without question, so their brains calmed down. At least as it related to food security.

That's what you're up against: a brain and body conditioned for survival, not safety.

HOW TO RESPOND

When you catch a kid sneaking food, your first instinct might be to clamp down. You want to teach them a lesson and show them who's in charge. Maybe you lock the fridge, take away their dessert, or, like my adoptive mom, force them to eat until they're sick. I get it—it feels like you're losing control, and you want to fix it. But here's the truth: That's a no-go zone.

---

18 U.S. Department of Justice, *Report of the Attorney General's National Task Force on Children Exposed to Violence*, December 12, 2012.

Punishment doesn't teach trust; it teaches fear. It tells the kid, "You're bad," and shame keeps them stuck in that survival rut. It also burns *your* emotional battery because now you're fighting a war nobody wins. I've seen foster parents get so drained by these battles that they start resenting the kid. It's not what you signed up for, and it's not what the kid needs.

So, let's talk about the go zone, the trauma-informed way to handle this. First, take a deep breath. Your tone is your superpower. When a kid is in survival mode, they can't process your words; they're too busy scanning for threats. But your tone? That cuts through the noise in their minds. Use a calm, steady voice, like you're soothing a scared puppy. Instead of demanding, "Why did you steal this?" try saying something like, "Hey, I see you're worried about food. Let's make sure you always have enough." Don't accuse, don't judge. You're not a cop—you're a coach.

Next, create abundance. Keep a bowl of healthy snacks—apples, granola bars, carrots—out in the open where the child can grab them anytime, no questions asked. This isn't about giving in. It's about showing their brain, "Food isn't a threat here." For a 4-year-old, make it fun: a colorful bowl with goldfish crackers or gummy fruit snacks. For a 15-year-old, stock protein bars or trail mix they can toss in their backpack. The message is the same: "You're safe. There's enough. No need to worry."

I worked with a foster mom in California who tried this with a 12-year-old boy who would hoard food. After a month of keeping a snack bowl stocked, he stopped hiding food in his room. Why? Possibly because his brain started to believe the famine was finally over. The consistency calmed the emotional drive and the access built a new behavior—everybody won.

You may say "I tried that. They just kept eating the food." That's the point! **QTIP—Quit Taking It Personally.** You don't know how the child will respond or how long it will take. They are conditioned by their own survival instincts, which may be counterproductive to your expectations.

Often, people try a suggested intervention like this and when the children don't immediately begin to respond as the adult thinks they should, the adults become microaggressive. Maybe they are tired and frustrated. They're expecting the kids to behave differently. It's as if the adults are asking the kid, "Why aren't you fixed yet?" Our brains just don't work that way. We have to try a tactic long enough for the child's brain to accept it as fact. If we change anything too soon, we risk interrupting the development of consistency and predictability in the child's brain.

Adults want to revert to controlling and commanding the situation because it's easier. Your facial expressions change, your vocal tone becomes one of disappointment. You may hate it when the kids roll their eyes, yet you are the first to respond exactly the same way. You probably don't notice how you're responding. So, do they believe your words or your body language?

Remember, 85% of our body language is unconscious: We are not aware it's even happening. But trauma has attuned your child to those very nonverbals for their safety and survival. They have been taught by their past that it is not about the words people say, but rather the behaviors that come afterward. They pay attention to your behavior, which gives them the best chance of avoiding being hurt again.

Another key is giving them control in a safe way. Trauma strips kids of control, so they grab it where they can—like sneaking food. Invite them into the kitchen. Let a younger kid pick between two veggies for dinner. Let a teen help plan a meal or tag along to the grocery store. This isn't just about food—it's about trust. When they feel like they have a say, they're less likely to fight for control in secret.

I remember a foster dad who started cooking with his 9-year-old foster daughter every Sunday. She was standoffish at first, but over time, she opened up, sharing stories while they chopped veggies. That's the go zone: connection, not control. (For more on this strategy, see *5 Reasons to Cook with Foster Kids* at www.CrummyMummy.co.uk.)

Finally, be patient. Trauma's a deep rut, and it takes repetition to carve a new path. Foster and adoptive kids experience two-and-a-half to three times the amount of violence exposure compared to kids from "good enough" homes. You're not going to fix this in a week. But every time you respond with unconditional regard—seeing the kid, not just the behavior—you're rewiring their brain for safety. You're also protecting your own heart. Don't waste your emotional energy on no-go zones like resentment or worrying about whether they'll "get it." Focus on the moment—on being the coach who shows up day after day.

Let's contrast this with a typical response. Say you catch a 10-year-old sneaking cookies. You might lecture them, "You know better! No dessert for a week." Or you lock the pantry, thinking it'll stop the behavior. What happens? The kid feels shamed, scared, and less likely to trust you. They might sneak more, hide it better, or shut down entirely. Now you're frustrated, they're defensive, and nobody's winning.

Compare that to a trauma-informed response: You find the cookies under their bed. You take a breath, kneel down, and say, "Hey, looks like you're making sure you have enough. Want to help me fill a snack bowl for your room?" You're not excusing the behavior—you're addressing the need. You're saying, "I see you, and I'm here." That's what starts to change things.

Of course, that's not where you want to end up, but it's a starting point. Your end goal may be that there is no food in bedrooms. Allowing safety to establish will often empower the child to make the choice to not have food in their room. And when that happens, everyone wins. Recognizing the process and working through small, slow steps forward gives the child's brain time to establish that you are safe and that their needs are being met.

That bridge takes patience, though, and you'll wobble if you try to cross it too quickly. Their tests can spark your doubt, tempting you to push or pull back. I've stumbled there, misreading a kid's fear and responding in ways that didn't build connection, but over time, I learned that curiosity and calm will keep you steady.

Here are some ways to respond when trust feels fragile, even if you're still learning the steps.

PRACTICAL TOOLS

These tools are designed to help you coach a kid through food insecurity, which is no different than teaching them to swing a bat or play a piano scale. It's about repetition, connection, and building trust. They're adaptable for kids of all ages because while the details change, the goal—safety and trust—stays the same.

Try these, tweak them, and keep going—even when it feels slow. You have to be a bit of a scientist. Every child is different; therefore, each one will respond differently. However, make sure it is NEVER rooted in shame, fear, or lack of trust. Boundaries and consequences are necessary, but these children are unaccustomed to healthy boundaries.

- **Snack bowl strategy**: Set up a bowl of healthy snacks in a common area—think apples, granola bars, or crackers. Tell the child, "This is always here for you, no matter what." Refill it regularly, even if they take a lot. For younger kids, make it inviting: a bright bowl with fun snacks like fruit snacks or cheese sticks. For teens, include grab-and-go options like protein bars or nuts. Check-in weekly to see what they like and involve them in restocking. This signals abundance and reduces the need to hoard. One foster mom I worked with noticed her 7-year-old stopped hiding food after two months of this—she'd finally started to believe there'd always be enough. Self-regulation is a learned behavior, which takes both time and a safe setting.

- **Coaching exercise—kitchen connection**: Invite the child to help with a food-related task once a week. For a young child, it could be stirring batter, picking a fruit, or setting the table. For a teen, maybe it's planning a meal, helping shop, or even cooking a side dish. Use this as a chance to connect, not lecture. Share a story about your favorite childhood food or a funny cooking mishap. Ask them what they like to eat and listen without judgment. This builds trust and gives them control in a safe way. There are many examples of this working well when we remain consistent. We, as caregivers, have to guard against misunderstanding the relationship between food and control for kids who have been deprived.

- **Grounding exercise—food journal**: For older kids (10–15), try a low pressure food journal. Give them a notebook and say, "When you feel worried about food, jot down what's going on. No rules, just write or draw." For younger kids (4–9), use a "feelings chart" with emojis (happy, scared, hungry) they can point to. This helps them name their anxiety without pressure. Review it together weekly not to judge, but to understand. If they're not ready to share, that's okay—keep offering. This teaches them to connect feelings to actions, a skill trauma often disrupts.

- **Journaling prompt for parents**: Reflect on a time you felt frustrated by a child's food behavior—hoarding, sneaking, refusing to eat, or overeating. Write down what happened, how you reacted, and how it felt in your body (e.g., tight chest, racing heart). Now, imagine the child's past: Were they hungry? Scared of scarcity? How might that explain their actions? List one way you could respond differently next time, like softening your tone, offering a snack without judgment, or inviting them to cook with you. Revisit this reflection after a week to see how your approach has shifted. This helps you move from reacting in the no-go zone (anger, control) to responding in the go zone (curiosity, connection), and protects your emotional energy.

- **Self-assessment**: Ask yourself, "Am I reacting to the behavior (with anger, control) or responding to the child's need for safety?" Rate your response on a scale of 1 to 5 (1 = reactive, 5 = trauma informed). List one small change you can make—like pausing to breathe or keeping a snack bowl stocked—to show unconditional regard. Revisit this weekly to track your progress.

These tools aren't a quick fix, but they're a start. You're not just feeding a kid's body; you're feeding their trust.

And trust? That's what rewires a brain for healing. Keep coaching, keep showing up, and know that every step you take is making a difference, even if you don't see it yet.

You've taken the first step—understanding *why* a foster child might hoard food and how to respond with love, not control. By staying in the go zone, you're building a foundation of trust that can change a kid's world. But what happens when that trust is tested by a different kind of challenge, like a child who screams or shuts down at the smallest trigger?

In the next chapter, we'll dive into the world of hypervigilance and emotional dysregulation—those moments when a kid's fear explodes into meltdowns or withdrawal. You'll hear another story from my childhood, learn why kids' brains can get stuck in panic mode, and get practical tools to calm the storm, helping both you and the child find peace in the chaos.

CHAPTER 4

The Screaming Child– Hypervigilance and Emotional Dysregulation

By the time I was 9 years old, I had been to four different schools. I had no childhood friends due to our constant moves. No consistency, no outlet. For me, school was a relief because home felt like a battlefield. And yet, I didn't know how to relate to other kids because I had this deep sense of shame, which was well established.

Because we moved so much, I got really good at lying to make myself look better. I was so used to walking on eggshells at home that I became hyperactive and kinetic when I got to school, always touching something or moving somehow. I would get in trouble all the time. Emotional dysregulation and my parents' heavy control response led to my inability to stop bouncing all over the place like popcorn as soon as I was free of their oversight.

I even got kicked out of Cub Scouts due to my uncontrollable behavior.

For another child, getting ready for school could be a battle not merely with you, the foster parents, but also with the child's own inner panic. The sound of the bus honking outside becomes like a siren in your child's head sending his heart racing and palms sweating. One day, it becomes too much. He bolts to his room, diving under the bed with raw, ragged screams emanating.

Often, this scenario is met with a parent who storms in yelling, "What's wrong with you? Get up, now! You're going to be late!" And yet, a child is often unable to explain their feelings. These sensations, these overpowering emotions, don't yet have words attached to them. All they know is that something feels wrong and dangerous, like the world is closing in. Your shouting only makes it worse. The child curls up tighter, screaming louder, until you're stuck with seemingly no recourse but to drag the child out and send them to school still shaking.

What you may have thought was defiant behavior was actually a sense of terror—your child's brain stuck in a loop of fear that they don't know how to shut off or explain.

If you've been a foster parent for a long time, you've probably seen something like this—a kid who loses it over something small like leaving for school, changing activities, or even a loud noise. Maybe it's a 6-year-old screaming and hiding during transitions, or a 14-year-old who melts down when you ask them to do their homework. It's exhausting, isn't it? You're trying to keep the day moving and suddenly, you're dealing with a full-blown crisis. You might feel helpless, frustrated, or angry, wondering why they can't just "get it together."

I'm here to tell you: It's not about you, and it's also not about them being "bad." It's about what trauma has done to their brain, keeping them on high alert, ready to fight or flee at the slightest trigger. When children (or anyone, for that matter) have been living in a constant state of fear, their brains learn to expect to be afraid. Their brains become wired toward anxiety and hypervigilance.

Let me break it down so you can respond in a way that calms the storm instead of adding to it.

I saw this firsthand during a consultation in Nebraska a few years back. A foster mom, we'll call her Lisa, shared a story about her 10-year-old adopted son. Every morning, getting him in the car to drop him off at school was like pulling teeth. He'd scream, kick, hide under the couch, crying, "I don't want to go!" Lisa tried everything—bribing him with snacks, threatening to take away his toys, even raising her voice to match his. When they would finally get to school, he wouldn't get out of the car. He would stubbornly sit in the back seat with his arms crossed, afraid to go into this school.

My first contact with him was as a witness as he sat in the back of the car. The police arrived and their presence was what got him out of the car and to the door of the school when he balked at the door. The police officer moved over him and loomed, which triggered a violent reaction, and he started to fight. The police officer responded to the boy's actions by subduing him and then taking him to the hospital for a psychiatric hold.

That is an unnecessary experience if the effects of trauma are understood, but that event became a case study for change within the agency. "When we know better, we do better," as Maya Angelou said.

THE SCIENCE

When a kid's been through trauma, abuse, neglect, or bouncing between homes, their brain gets rewired to expect danger. Picture a light switch flipped to "on" and jammed there. That's the amygdala, the brain's threat detector, constantly shouting, "Watch out! Something's coming!" This is called hypervigilance. It's like living with a smoke alarm that goes off every time you so much as toast bread! For foster kids, everyday moments like leaving for school, hearing a raised voice, or even a change in routine can feel like a five-alarm fire.

When the amygdala is so sensitive, it drowns everything else out. The fear of being hurt shuts down so many parts of the brain that what they are learning is impacted, which only adds to their frustration. Their inability to do what is asked is confounding and shame producing. The child is often already punishing themselves long before you get upset because they still haven't put on their shoes or brushed their teeth.

Their brain hits the panic button, and they react with screams, hiding, or shutting down not because they want to, but because their body thinks it's a matter of survival. Transitions are the worst, going from what is real right in front of you to going to a place you can't see and don't know what's there. Terrifying for a kid who feels alone.

Here's how it works. Early trauma, especially in the first few years of life, disrupts the brain's ability to regulate emotions. Normally, a secure attachment with a caregiver teaches a kid's brain how to calm down and trust that things will be okay even when they are scared. But when that attachment is broken or nonexistent, their brain has to learn to self-soothe. In this developmental phase, the coaching of a good-enough caregiver promotes co-regulation and connection. In an unhealthy environment, with an uncaring or disconnected caregiver, the infant is not getting the consistent, nurturing, loving interactions they need to develop healthy attachment. They are neglected or suffer through hostile interactions where they have to learn to self-soothe. At their deepest emotional core, they have already learned that "no one is coming."

When they cry out, no one comes. When they are hungry, no one comes. Cold, lonely, alone, the emotional brain gets built in a way that does not know how to tolerate vulnerability, and it's not their fault. They have no words for it. So, when a kid is screaming or hiding, they're not *choosing* to act out. They're stuck in a survival loop, and their brain is saying, "Run! Fight! Protect yourself!"

The most common **founded abuse** (proven in court, probably the reason this child is in your care) for children is infant neglect. How does a child communicate that to you? In the only way they know how: through behavior that makes us uncomfortable to witness. And it's not their fault.

Remember my story of when I was a kid in Panama, running around barefoot until I stepped on a piece of glass? I was more afraid of my parents' response than the pain of cutting my foot open. Kids will put up with a lot of internal pain to avoid the shame of being told—again—that there's something wrong with them. This is an example of shame that translates into immobilization. A child may stand frozen due to the yelling, while the parent gets more and more frustrated. And the child becomes more and more frozen.

This is our primal brain in action: "If I remain frozen, I won't be seen by the lion." Constant threat becomes their norm, their expectation, and their brain becomes wired through fear.

Remember, **criticism without connection is rejection**. The way I have been taught by so many kids is that they "don't belong." The tapes that play in their minds say things like, "I am not good enough, so you will give me away too." For many kids, connection has to come before constructive criticism can begin.

When a foster kid lands in your home, their brain is caught in a storm, drowning out their words. I tell parents: Think of a time you were so overwhelmed—maybe a deadline or loss— that your thoughts felt submerged. That's a foster kid's daily life, not just a moment. Their brain is a locked gate, shaped by trauma, and blocks their ability to explain feelings, leaving "I don't know" as their only response.

Judith Herman notes kids rely on "an immature system of psychological defenses."[19] I see this in so many kids in the beginning, "You don't know me", "Why am I here", "Can I go now?" Your calm presence, rather than questions, starts

---

19 Judith L. Herman, *Trauma and Recovery: The Aftermath of Violence—from Domestic Abuse to Political Terror*, 2nd ed. (New York: Basic Books, 2015), 96.

to quiet that internal storm. That storm keeps their nervous system on edge, ready to react. By offering safety and calm, you help their brain settle, setting the stage for trust.

There's another piece to this: the nervous system. Trauma leaves a kid's nervous system charged up with tension, ready to discharge at any moment. This is why small triggers—a loud voice, an unexpected change—can set off a big reaction. It's not just the moment—it's all the moments before, stored in their body, waiting to explode.

That's what hypervigilance does: It turns the world into a threat, and the kid's brain reacts *before* they can think.

But here's the hope: The brain is malleable, meaning it is flexible. In the brain-science world, we use the term "neuroplasticity" to describe the way in which our brains can change as we learn and grow. Every time you respond with calm and safety, you're helping that kid's amygdala dial down. You're teaching their nervous system: "Hey, you can relax. This is a safe place." It's not instant. It takes repetition, like learning to play an instrument. But every calm response is a note in the song of healing. That's why how you respond matters so much.

You're not just managing a meltdown; you're creating the safe environment that allows the child's brain to rewire for trust.

HOW TO RESPOND

When a kid is screaming, hiding, or melting down, your first instinct might be to match their energy. You raise your voice, demand they stop, or send them to their room to "calm down." I get it—it's human to react when you're stressed, and a screaming kid is like a siren going off in your own brain. But that's a no-go zone.

Yelling, punishing, or isolating a kid in a meltdown tells their brain, "You're not safe," and it escalates the fear. It also drains *your* emotional battery because now you're in a power struggle, fighting a kid who's not even fighting you because instead they are fighting their own panic.

I've seen foster parents get so burned out from these battles that they start pulling away, resenting the kid who, once again, becomes the scapegoat, held responsible for the effects of what happened to them. That's not what you signed up for, and it's not what the kid needs. When a kid is in a meltdown, their brain can't process words. That part of the brain is offline; they're too busy surviving.

Let's talk about the go zone, the trauma-informed way to handle this.

First, take a deep breath. Seriously, do it now. Your calm is your superpower. Instead of "stop screaming!" try, "Hey, I'm here. You're safe." Use a soft, steady voice, like you're talking to a scared animal. Don't demand answers or explanations—they can't give them yet. Your job is to signal safety, to be the anchor in their storm.

Next, help them ground. This means bringing their brain back to the present moment, away from the panic. For a younger kid, try something tactile, like holding their hand or offering a soft blanket. For an older kid, guide them to notice their surroundings: "Can you name three things you see right now?"

This isn't about fixing the meltdown—it's about telling their brain: "You're okay."

Create predictability. Trauma makes the world feel chaotic, so routines are like a lifeline. Use visual schedules (pictures for younger kids and written lists for teens) to make transitions less unexpected and scary. When the unknown becomes known, fear disappears. Involve the kid in making the schedule, so they feel some control. Kids are fighting for some control anyway; it is a natural developmental process. Holding good boundaries is also necessary. Often, when working with kids in any structured setting, our compassion can turn into enabling. If the kids are designing the day, if they are able to influence you to change things, who is actually in control of the setting?

Stay steady. Growing up in uncertainty is most often going to result in impulsivity and reactivity. Around 1970, at the child care center at Stanford, they did a delayed gratification experiment which eventually became known as "The marshmallow test."[20] They put children in a room with a marshmallow and the instructions were that if the marshmallow was uneaten when they came back in 15 minutes, then they would get another marshmallow.

They are still monitoring those kids as grownups today. They have found that at each developmental milestone, the kids who delayed eating the marshmallow reached the milestone sooner than those who could not wait for the delayed gratification.

---

20 Walter Mischel, Ebbe B. Ebbesen, and Andera Raskoff Zeiss, "Cognitive and Attentional Mechanisms in Delay of Gratification," *Journal of Personality and Social Psychology* 21, no. 2 (1972): 204–18, https://doi.org/10.1037/h0032198.

Up until this experiment, most people assumed that impulsivity was innate; some kids were just born that way. But later experiments showed it was likely that impulsivity was environmentally conditioned in under-resourced households.

So, if children are conditioned that someone won't calm their chaos overnight, meltdowns will test you. But every soft question, like "light on or off?" shows you're a safe anchor instead of another storm. Small steps stabilize kids, building trust one moment at a time. Don't drain yourself chasing quick fixes or resentment. It's your steady presence that holds space for their healing and yours. Those small steps set the stage for responding to big reactions without breaking trust. When a kid's fear erupts, your calm can be their lifeline, not another trigger.

Let's contrast this with a typical response. Say your 6-year-old foster son is screaming because it's time to leave for school. You might yell, "Enough! Get in the car!" or drag him out, thinking it'll teach him to listen. What happens? His panic spikes, his trust in you drops, and he's more likely to melt down again tomorrow. You're frustrated, he's scared, and you're both stuck.

The trauma-informed response: You find him hiding under the table, screaming. You take a breath, lower yourself to his level and say, "Hey, I see you're scared. I'm right here. Let's take some deep breaths together." You model slow breathing, maybe offer a favorite toy. You're not excusing the behavior—you're addressing the fear. You're saying, "I see you, and you're safe."

Another example: In consultation with a residential program, I met a 13-year-old child who was in and out of homes in the area. He struggled with violent outbursts and relentless persecution from those he perceived were against him. I met him one day, and we began chatting as he held a deck of cards. I asked him what games he liked to play and in no time, we were playing Hearts.

As we played, I showed him how to cut the deck of cards with one hand. He was fascinated, so I walked him through it. He began to practice with great focus and before long, it was time for me to leave. I told him I would be back in a week, and I couldn't wait to see how well he was cutting the cards. I came back the next week and when I walked onto his floor, he was in front of me instantly.

He proudly held the deck in his hand, and I said "Let's see it." He proudly and slowly cut the deck with one hand. I high fived him and complimented him on his success. The staff member next to me then muttered, "Oh, now you think you are big stuff because you can cut a deck of cards."

It was triggering for me as a professional as I remembered my own childhood humiliation. But as that moment was not about me, I quickly recovered and watched this young man become overwhelmed by shame. His shame turned to rage, and he flung the cards on the ground, stormed to his room, so deeply hurt in a moment of vulnerability. The staff member was oblivious as to how he had impacted the child. I walked over to the kid's door, told him I was proud, and I would be there when he was ready to talk.

While I was able to talk to him eventually, he targeted that staff member relentlessly the entire time he was in that residential program. He screamed and threw things whenever that person was present. It took time to help people understand what had happened from the kid's point of view, including the foster family, but over the time I knew him, he was learning to manage his emotions when he was with safe adults. One sarcastic comment destroyed any opportunity that the staff member may have had to build a connection with this boy.

All of this takes time and patience on your part. Until you have the habit, it's not going to occur to you to do something. But how do you build a habit? Consistency, permission to learn, and mentoring toward learning. Their pushback is normal and not a reason to give up. Persevere.

When you introduce a new concept, you have to engage that individual at least 10 to 12 times to make it familiar, and each of these repetitions must be positive in order to begin building a healthy expectation. Human brains need to hear a new thing at least five to six times before we begin to perceive it as important to learn. And THEN we need to hear it at least another five to six times before we begin to attempt to apply it.

If you begin to experience frustration during those 10 to 12 times, then you're triggering the wrong part of their brains, and they are not receiving what you want them to get. Repetition, continuous reminders of our purpose, and reaffirmation of its importance.

PRACTICAL TOOLS

These tools are your playbook for coaching a kid through hypervigilance and meltdowns, like teaching them to swing a bat or play a song. It's about repetition, connection, and building trust. They're adaptable for kids at every age and developmental stage because while the details change, the goal—safety and trust—stays the same. Try these, tweak them, and keep going, even when it feels slow.

- **Grounding exercise**: 5–4–3–2–1. Teach the child this technique during a calm moment, so it's familiar when a meltdown hits. Say, "Let's play a game. Name five things you see, four things you can touch, three things you hear, two things you smell, one thing you taste." For younger kids, simplify it: "What do you see? What do you feel?" For teens, they may want to lead the exercise, or maybe they would rather write their thoughts down. Practice weekly, making it fun, like a scavenger hunt. Then when a meltdown occurs, they are already trained in a healthy response. You can guide them more quickly because they are already accustomed to this pattern: "Can you tell me one thing you see?" This pulls their brain back to the present. A foster mom I trained used this with her 7-year-old and, after a month, he'd start the exercise himself when he felt overwhelmed.

- **Coaching exercise**: visual schedule. Create a visual schedule for daily transitions, like morning routines or bedtime. For younger kids, use pictures (e.g., a toothbrush, a bus). For teens, use a written list or app. Involve the child in designing it—let them draw or pick colors. Review it daily, celebrating small wins (e.g., "You followed the schedule—awesome!"). This builds predictability and control.

- **Calm corner strategy**: Set up a cozy corner in your home—a beanbag, blankets, and soft toys—where the child can go when they're overwhelmed. Introduce it during a calm moment: "This is your safe spot whenever you need it." For younger kids, add sensory items like a glitter jar. For teens, include headphones or a journal. Don't force them to use it—just make it available.
- **Storytelling exercise—safe moments**: Share a story about a time you felt safe or calm, modeling vulnerability. For a 4-year-old, it might be, "I love snuggling with my dog—it makes me feel cozy." For a 15-year-old, share a memory of a peaceful hike. Then gently ask, "Do you have a moment when you felt calm?" Don't push—just plant the seed. This builds connection and helps them identify safety.
- **Journaling prompt for parents**: Reflect on a time when a child's meltdown, screaming, hiding, or lashing out triggered your frustration. Write down what happened, how you reacted, and how it felt. Now, imagine the child's past: Were they scared? Unsafe? How might that explain their behavior? List one way you could respond differently next time, like lowering your tone or offering a grounding exercise, to stay in the go zone. This helps you shift from reaction to curiosity, protecting your emotional energy.
- **Self-assessment**: Ask yourself: "Am I reacting to the meltdown (with anger, control) or responding to the child's need for safety?" Rate your response on a scale of 1 to 5 (1 = reactive, 5 = trauma informed). List one small change you can make—like pausing to breathe or using a

visual schedule—to show unconditional regard. Revisit this weekly to track your progress.

These tools aren't a magic wand, but they're a start. You're not just calming a meltdown; you're teaching a kid's brain what safety feels like. And trust? That's what builds a bridge to healing. Keep coaching, keep showing up, and know that every moment you choose the go zone is making a difference, even if it's hard to see.

We've talked about how to navigate the storm of a foster child's meltdowns by using calm and connection to help their brain find safety. By choosing the go zone of patience, grounding, and routines, you're building trust that can weather even the toughest moments. But what happens when that trust is challenged in a different setting and you're not there to shape your child's reaction?

In the next chapter, we'll explore school-based challenges. You'll hear another story from my childhood, uncover why school can be such a place of fear and reprisal, and get practical tools to foster honesty and connection, strengthening the bond you're working so hard to create.

CHAPTER 5

The School Struggle–Trauma in Educational Settings

School can be a minefield for foster kids where their trauma responses tend to show up as disruption, withdrawal, or defiance, which are often misunderstood by teachers and principals. As a foster parent, you might have to advocate fiercely not only with the school to create trauma-informed support but also with your child, helping them navigate classrooms and peer interactions without shame or fear.

This chapter gives you the science, stories, and strategies to bridge the gap between a child's fear-built brain and a school system that is built for compliance rather than healing. You'll learn to partner with educators, empower your child, and push for environments where they can connect, play, and thrive—not just survive.

MY STORY: A KID MISUNDERSTOOD

At age 9, I was a whirlwind in every school I attended, frequently labeled "trouble" for lying to fit in or for bouncing around the classroom because I was overwhelmed. There was too much stimulation, too many new kids, and I didn't know how to fit in using the tactics I had available to me.

In those days, they didn't have Special Education (SPED) classrooms. Teachers tended to give overactive kids like me a seat right up front, under their watchful eye. SPED refers to tailored educational programs and services designed to meet the unique needs of students with disabilities or behavioral challenges to ensure they receive appropriate support to succeed academically and socially.

My behavior in those days tended toward the spotlight. I was impulsive, looking for any opportunity to perform, to get giggles, to be liked—a class clown. In the sixth grade, still on the path to becoming a priest in my adopted parents' eyes, I was serving Mass as an altar boy, cleaning the convent on weekends, and attending Catholic school. Then one day, I was challenged by a boy in class to fight. We met after school; I had been boxing for three years and bloodied his nose immediately. The Mother Superior came around the corner at that instant and informed me that I was through at that school and so were my younger siblings. We were expelled.

I was rejected once again, and yet the other kid was not expelled—even though he initiated the fight. That lack of justice wasn't lost on me, nor was the punishment I received when the principal's call came that night. I still remember the fear that held me frozen, as my siblings and I sat at the top of the stairs, listening to my father's side of that call. Punished again, even though it wasn't my fault.

You want to see something disheartening? Go into any SPED classroom in most school districts. I have seen a couple of good ones, but most are rooms of resentment and subversion as the kids distract themselves from their shame and rejection by either acting out, causing disruptions, or hiding within themselves, dissociating from their environment.

Due to constant underfunding, these classrooms tend to become chaotic environments with a staff that generally lack training in trauma-informed principles. Most school districts have merely created rooms where children who have been labeled by the "system," as having survived difficult childhood challenges, are warehoused Monday through Friday, 7:30 a.m. to 2:30 p.m., until they are 18 years old or they quit showing up.

These students' brains, which were designed to adapt to their chaotic home environments, are now measured in school based on the behavioral expectations developed in calm and safety. The brain that was built in survival amidst chaos is now impulsive and environmentally reactive.

Then they get to school and are labeled a "bad kid," or given a diagnosis like ADHD, dissociative disorder, or borderline personality disorder. They are aware of, and reactive to, nonverbal social cues that tell them they are *different*. Students and teachers alike are caught in this negative feedback cycle where one acts and another reacts, which triggers an ever escalating reaction. Eventually, violence explodes and a student is expelled, or worse.

Instead of honoring their strength, we continue the victimization in the school setting. Instead of providing the missing pieces of childhood that would allow them to experience safety, calmness, and prosocial connectedness, we too often reinforce the school-to-prison pipeline.

This pipeline isn't just a metaphor; it's a one-way trap that funnels traumatized kids from classrooms to courtrooms, turning survival instincts into criminal records. Studies show that foster kids with high ACE (Adverse Childhood Experiences) scores are three times more likely to end up in juvenile justice not because they're "bad," but because schools treat their reactions as crimes rather than what they actually are: cries for help.[21]

But you can interrupt this pipeline. As a foster parent, your voice in school meetings, advocating for your child with suggestions like "Let's try ARC (Attachment, Regulation, Competency) or a calm corner," can shift the conversation to support, keeping kids in classrooms instead of cells. It's not easy, but it's possible. Start small. Share this book with a teacher or advocate for district-wide trauma training. Your love can break the cycle, turning a "bad kid" into a thriving young person. You're enough for that fight.

THE SCIENCE: TRAUMA IN THE CLASSROOM

The pediatric version of JAMA (Journal of the American Medical Association) published a study that showed children who grow up in impoverished homes *lose* gray matter in some

---

21 A. D. Engler et al., "A Systematic Review of Mental Health Disorders of Children in Foster Care," Trauma, Violence, & Abuse 23, no. 1 (2022): 255–64, https://doi.org/10.1177/1524838020941197.

regions of the brain compared to kids who grow up in good enough homes.[22]

The brain is a "use it or lose it" tool, but this doesn't mean that it has to be permanent. The brain has immense plasticity at that age with the right workarounds or adjustments. Think of how an occupational or physical therapist might retrain the body to adapt to a missing limb, for example.

The brain can make beautiful adaptations. But when adults in authority don't know how to respond, they often swing wildly between harsh punishments and pity driven permissiveness. That inconsistency—yelling one day and letting it slide the next—leaves kids on edge and unable to predict what's coming. It keeps them locked in fear and survival, far from the trust they need to learn and grow. Consistent discipline, however, is different. It's not about control; it's a steady rhythm that says, "I'm here, and you're safe, even when you mess up."

Parents and teachers who hold firm but loving boundaries build that predictability, helping the child's brain shift from chaos to calm. Over time, this trust becomes the foundation for their highest potential, turning a kid who freezes in class into one who raises their hand, or a yeller into a problem solver. I've seen it in foster homes where a simple "two-minute cooldown" rule, enforced with a calm "let's breathe together," transformed meltdowns into moments of connection.

Trauma overwhelms working memory, making it hard for kids to follow instructions or remember lessons, especially

---

22 Nicole L. Hair et al., "Association of Child Poverty, Brain Development, and Academic Achievement," *JAMA Pediatrics* 169, no. 9 (2015): 822–29, https://doi.org/10.1001/jamapediatrics.2015.1475.

in chaotic settings.[23] Stress hormones, like cortisol, flood the brain, blocking focus and emotional control.[24] This isn't about kids being "bad" or "slow." It's about a brain built to survive, not to solve equations.

The ACEs study, done by Dr. Vincent Felitti and colleagues in 1998, shows how tough childhoods—like abuse, neglect, or family chaos—pile up to hurt kids' brains and bodies.[25] Think of ACEs as heavy rocks in a kid's backpack. Each one (like a parent's addiction or moving to another new foster home) adds weight, making it harder to run, play, or learn. The study found that kids with more ACEs face bigger struggles with memory, attention, and emotions because their brains' stress system is stuck on high.

For foster kids, who often have multiple ACEs, school tasks like reading or sitting still can feel impossible. Their brain is overwhelmed by stress, hindering focus on tasks like spelling.

I see this in nearly every school I go to: children enduring a room full of judgment, trying to figure out how to connect with the other kids. They are using the brain that has worked for them, but that brain doesn't understand the academic information that is being presented, which fosters a sense of

---

23 National Child Traumatic Stress Network (NCTSN), Child Trauma Toolkit for Educators (Los Angeles, CA: NCTSN, 2018), 12, https://www.nctsn.org/resources/child-trauma-toolkit-educators.

24 Bessel A. van der Kolk, *The Body Keeps the Score: Brain, Mind, and Body in the Healing of Trauma* (New York: Viking, 2014), 97.

25 Vincent J. Felitti et al., "Relationship of Childhood Abuse and Household Dysfunction to Many of the Leading Causes of Death in Adults: The Adverse Childhood Experiences (ACE) Study," *American Journal of Preventive Medicine* 14, no. 4 (1998): 245–58, https://doi.org/10.1016/S0749-3797(98)00017-8.

shame and expectation of failure that gets in the way of trying to learn.

Healthy socialization turbocharges good academics for most kids. If a kid knows who they belong to, they are more comfortable and relaxed in the world. Without connection, the child feels alone and often spends more time and energy suppressing the expression of fear, even though it dominates them internally. This makes it nearly impossible for them to listen and comprehend the instructions of the teacher.

Their brain and other parts of the central nervous system are struggling to carry those rocks, which hinders the child's ability to focus on spelling. I see this with many of the preteens I work with. They have become good at avoiding schoolwork—and the overwhelming shame and judgment that comes with being put in the spotlight for their poor academics.

The system has failed them and academic hopelessness sets in. Knowing about ACEs matters because it can show you why your kid struggles and help you advocate for school support, like extra time or quieter spaces, to lighten their load. Reminder: It is not the kids fault. They are often as bewildered as you are. They can't articulate what is happening to them. How overwhelming that must be!

In a bustling third grade classroom in a Midwestern school, a boy was unraveling. He'd sweep everything off his desk—books, pencils, laptop—before turning to disrupt other kids' belongings. His outbursts were a storm, chaotic and unsettling for everyone. The school asked me to help them make a plan. Digging deeper, I learned the boy's father had recently been deported, and his older brother was relentlessly tormenting him at home. When the boy acted out, his teacher's response, looming over the boy's desk, only triggered worse behavior because the looming figure echoed his sense of threat.

Looming (standing over someone else in a threatening manner) works for most kids in that it *suppresses* unwanted behavior. But at what cost? The child's brain absorbs the looming as a threat, which harms rather than strengthens connection with the adult. A well-integrated third grader will shake it off fairly easily, but most kids will become progressively uneasy.

I realized that the boy's actions weren't just defiance; they were a cry from a brain overwhelmed by stress and loss. The school had created a simple plan: clear the classroom during outbursts to remove the boy's "audience," which they thought was fueling his disruptions. However, this created major disruption in the learning environment for the rest of the students.

After some observation, I introduced a white 3 x 5 card placed on the boy's desk. When the boy felt overwhelmed, he could hold up the card, signaling a teacher's aide to take him for a short walk or a quick game before returning to class. Knowing kids in distress often can't recall such tools in the heat of the moment, I trained the aide to proactively approach the boy twice per class session, hold up the card, and offer a break. This built a pattern of safety before the boy even needed it.

A month later, some staff grumbled, claiming the boy was "manipulating" the system and not learning. I then asked the simple question, "How many times have you had to clear the classroom this month?" The answer: none. The other students were learning without disruptions, and the boy was getting his needs met through a consistent, predictable routine that felt like a secure attachment. Within a couple of months, he only raised the card once or twice a day, down from multiple times per class period. He was learning to recognize his own overwhelm and able to access safety, expanding his ability to handle challenges throughout the school day.

The real story, though, lies beneath. Some teachers saw the boy's progress as "getting his way," revealing their own biases when a child's needs took priority over the teacher's "control" in the classroom.

But who was truly winning? Not only the boy, who found safety instead of rejection, but also the whole classroom, which could now focus. Redefining "winning" meant prioritizing the boy's sense of control and security by teaching him and the adults that meeting a child's needs transforms everyone's experience. For foster parents, this underscores the power of advocating for trauma-informed strategies that build safety and connection, allowing kids to thrive despite their heavy burdens.

School can feel like a stormy sea for foster kids, their trauma tossing them like waves against the rocks of tests, rules, and crowded hallways. Their brains, wired for survival, don't switch to "learn mode" when the bell rings. Instead, they're scanning for threats—loud voices, a teacher's sharp tone, or a classmate's shove.

Schools often miss this. They're built on a "mentalist model," a fancy term for a big mistake, expecting every kid to have a calm, ready-to-learn brain, like some factory standard model.

Picture a teacher handing out a test, assuming every kid's brain is a clear desk, ready to work. But your foster kid's desk is cluttered with trauma's chaos—fear, shame, or memories of loss. When they act out or zone out, schools label them "disruptive" or "unmotivated," not seeing the survival wiring underneath. I coached a foster dad whose 8-year-old son, Jay, got detentions for "not listening" during science. Jay's home life, bouncing between foster homes, meant his brain saw the teacher's rapid-fire questions as threats, not challenges.

The mentalist model ignores the reality of these children's brain development, judging kids against a brain they don't have. It's like asking a kid with a broken leg to run a race, then punishing them for falling. Schools, designed 120 years ago to churn out factory workers, lean on outdated tools, like detentions and behavior charts, which only deepen trauma's wiring. They're bailing water from a sinking boat without patching the holes.

There's a better way: the **ARC model**, which stands for *Attachment, Regulation,* and *Competency*. It's like a three-legged stool to steady your kid in school. First, **Attachment** builds trust through safe, consistent relationships. A teacher who greets your kid warmly, saying, "Glad you're here," helps their brain feel safe. Second, **Regulation** teaches kids to calm their emotions, like deep breathing when they're overwhelmed. Third, **Competency** gives them skills, like breaking math into small steps, so they feel capable, not defeated. ARC emphasizes secure relationships (attachment), emotional regulation (e.g., breathing exercises), and skill building (e.g., problem solving), adaptable for any child.

Blaustein and Kinniburgh say ARC rewires trauma's chaos by meeting kids where they are, not where schools expect them to be.[26] You can advocate for this—ask teachers for five-minute breaks or a consistent buddy to build trust. It's not a quick fix, but it turns school from a stormy sea into a safe harbor.

Your advocacy is the key. When you explain ACEs to a teacher—"My kid's carrying a heavy load from their past"—you shift their lens from "bad kid" to "hurting kid." When you push for ARC strategies, like a quiet space or a check in, you're helping rewire their brain for learning. You don't need a PhD to do this—just your voice and persistence. I've messed up plenty, but each mess up was a learning experience. Every calm conversation you have with a teacher, every small win like a breathing break, builds a bridge from threat to opportunity. You're enough for that.

WHAT YOU SEE

In school, trauma looks like a kid who can't sit still, talks back, or stares blankly at a worksheet, hiding under desks and trying to escape the pressure of too much stimulation. Other kids might hoard pencils (response to scarcity), lie about homework (to avoid shame), or lash out at peers (a desire to feel in control). These aren't "bad behaviors," but survival strategies, shaped by a past where trust was a trap.

QTIP: Quit Taking It Personally. When the school calls about "disrespect," it's not about you or the school—it's the child's trauma reacting to the perception of an unsafe system. Your

---

26 Margaret E. Blaustein and Kristine M. Kinniburgh, *Treating Traumatic Stress in Children and Adolescents* (New York: The Guilford Press, 2010), 145–47.

role is to see their fear, not their "failure," and advocate for a school that does the same. Not taking it personally will allow curiosity. If we look at it from the kids perspective, defiance can be a strength when given the right coaching. Suppression and punishment won't open the door to connection, nor will they promote real respect, gratitude, and empathy—qualities that we reward kids for in social settings but neglect to teach those qualities when lacking.

HOW TO RESPOND

Typical Response

When a foster kid struggles in school, it's easy to fall into blaming them—"Why can't you just behave?"—or accepting the school's punitive measures, like suspensions or detentions. These deepen shame, reinforcing the child's belief that they're "bad." Foster parents might feel caught, defending their kid while facing pressure to comply with school rules. This approach fails because it ignores trauma's role, triggering more fear and disconnection.

Trauma-Informed Response

A trauma-informed response begins with advocacy, both with the school and for your child. Collaborate with teachers to create plans that honor trauma's impact, like quiet corners for self-regulation or check ins before transitions.

For younger kids, if a child can't tolerate the classroom environment all the time, engage them in collaborative play, modeling strategies for managing stress. For example: "Whew, this is hard, I need to take a few deep breaths to focus better." For teens, teach self-advocacy skills, like asking, "Can I step out for a minute?" without fear.

Educate the school: IEPs (Individualized Education Programs) and behavior plans often set big goals—like "focus in class" or "follow instructions"—but overlook the step-by-step journey to get there, especially for kids whose brains are wired for survival, not sitting still. Push for trauma-informed tweaks, like short breaks or a buddy system, to make the path smoother. Use the ARC model (Attachment, Regulation, Competency), designed for complex trauma, to guide these plans. ARC focuses on building secure relationships (attachment), teaching emotional calming (regulation, e.g., deep breathing), and developing skills (competency, e.g., problem-solving), making it adaptable for any child's needs in school.[27]

An example of a program that works well when done right is SOAR (Strategies for Organization, Activation, and Regulation), a research-based learning system from SOAR Learning, Inc.[28] It helps kids build study skills through structured, flexible settings tailored to their needs, whether in small groups, one-on-one, or self-paced online modules. SOAR's mission emphasizes empowering students with tools for success, reducing overwhelm by breaking tasks into manageable steps—perfect for foster kids whose trauma

---

27 Margaret E. Blaustein and Kathleen M. Kinniburgh, *Treating Traumatic Stress in Children and Adolescents: A Comprehensive Overview and Comprehensive Workbook*, 2nd ed. (New York: Guilford Press, 2018), 145–47.

28 SOAR Learning, Inc., "About SOAR Learning, Inc.," SOAR Learning, accessed December 17, 2025, https://studyskills.com/about-soar/.

scatters focus. Schools can integrate it into IEPs to boost confidence and retention, turning "I can't" into "I got this."

Coaches and teachers will appreciate Brain Gym once they understand how the brain needs simple physical movements to stimulate focus and grit. Brain Gym is a set of 26 movements, designed to enhance coordination, attention, and emotional regulation through easy exercises like cross-crawls or hooking thumbs.[29] It's not therapy—it's a quick brain "warm-up," like stretching before a run, helping kids shake off hypervigilance and engage. Pair it with *Bal-a-vis-x*, a rhythm-based curriculum within Brain Gym, using balls, vision exercises, and balance tasks to build neural pathways for concentration and calm.[30] (Additional information is available at the end of this book in the Resources section.)

These tools aren't magic, but they meet kids where they are, turning chaotic classrooms into places of growth. However, no tool will ultimately work unless it is implemented repeatedly until it becomes part of the school culture.

Example: You have built a good relationship with your child. That child has a teacher or paraeducator they like at school or at an independent learning center. Trust and relationships need to be established first. Then, you need to know what the child's capacity is. If they are in the sixth grade but only read at a third grade level, then stop rationalizing, take a deep breath, and start where they are.

---

29 Paul E. Dennison and Gail E. Dennison, *Brain Gym: Simple Activities for Whole Brain Learning*, rev. ed. (Edu-K, 2010), 15–20.

30 Bal-A-Vis-X, Inc., "Bal-A-Vis-X Overview," Bal-A-Vis-X, accessed December 17, 2025, https://bal-a-vis-x.com/.

We can't magically make the brain understand words and context just because it would make it easier on us. **Quit Taking It Personally (QTIP)!** It's about helping your child move forward. With progressive success and an encouraging tutor who understands that the brain needs short academic doses in the beginning, while the brain forges new neural networks, then building on success begins to produce hope and confidence in that skill and for the future. Remember, the brain is a muscle too. When working new muscles, they can run out of gas quickly until they get enough repetition to be strong.

Teach your child how to advocate for themselves. Role-playing scenarios—just like our third grader and the paraprofessional, teach advocacy. When a child has been dismissed for most of their lives, their control taken away. They may have never been rewarded for sticking up for themselves—possibly punished for it in controlling environments—so it is a frozen part of their *self*, their understanding of who they are as individuals that needs to be thawed out and warmed up.

Give kids permission to play, not just perform. Interventions like Rainbowdance (see the Resources section, at the end of this book, for more information on this fantastic intervention program), a classroom-based program, let kids move, connect, and tell stories, reducing hypervigilance. Structured play and other activities and interventions foster peer trust through collaborative challenges. Good peer relationships quiet the negative brain, promote integration, and turbocharge academic absorption. Be a scientist: observe what triggers your child (e.g., group work, loud bells) and tailor strategies toward solutions. If the school resists, keep pushing—your advocacy is their lifeline.

I once worked with a ninth grader in a school who could not sit still. Every part of his body was in constant motion. I asked him what his interests were, and he said he was a NASCAR fan. But he quickly exclaimed that he could never be a driver.

"Look at me," he said, "I can't focus." We talked for a bit and I asked him what his favorite track was, and he talked about the famous tracks and the straightaways and turns. I asked him if he was willing to try something and he agreed.

I put my hand on the desk and counted to five without moving my hand. I asked him if he thought he could do it. He put his hand on the desk across from mine, and we counted to five. His hand stayed still even though his upper arm and shoulder were jerking. I remarked with wonder, "WOW! Did you see your arm jerking and yet you kept your hand still?" He was so proud. I challenged him to try both hands and again he was successful despite the shoulder and other body parts moving.

It was so cool to watch! I then asked him how long it takes to get through a turn in NASCAR, and he connected the dots immediately. "I can get through the turn!"

Here is a useful formula that I learned from my mentor, Robert Macy:

1. Attachment trajectory: What do they like?
2. Ask them to teach you about what they like. They get to be the expert.
3. Use that to create an activity they can use to reach a goal.

4. Chunk practice in doses they can tolerate, then repeat, repeat, repeat.

PRACTICAL TOOLS

Here are some tools to advocate for your foster child in school, blending science and heart:

- **Advocacy exercise**: Draft a letter to the school using the National Child Traumatic Stress Network (NCTSN) as a guide. Explain your child's trauma needs (e.g., "Loud voices trigger his fear response") and suggest solutions (e.g., "A quiet corner helps him regulate"). Keep it collaborative: "Let's work together for his success." Sample: "Dear Ms. Smith, My foster son, Marcus, has experienced trauma that makes classrooms feel unsafe. I have attached a fact sheet from the NCTSN for you. Can we discuss a plan with breaks or check ins to support his learning?"
- **Coaching exercise**: Role play a school scenario with your child. For a younger child, practice saying, "I'm feeling overwhelmed. Can I take a break?" For a teen, try, "I didn't mean to snap. I just need a moment." This builds confidence.
- **Journaling prompt**: Reflect on a recent school challenge (e.g., a call about "disrespect"). Write: "How might trauma shape my child's reaction? What's one trauma-informed step I can take?" Example: "Marcus yelled at his teacher. Maybe he felt trapped. I'll suggest a fidget toy for class." A fidget is only the first dose of tension management. To get masterful in the setting, there has to be a progression

that every teacher and coach is trained in. They need to already understand this from a curriculum or coaching perspective. Understanding how it applies to survival behavior is critical for a healthy school environment.

- **Self-assessment**: Are you advocating for trauma-informed practices? List one action, like requesting an ARC-based IEP meeting or sharing NCTSN's *Creating Trauma-Informed Schools* with the principal (see appendix).

- **Scattergraph tool**: Plot your approach on a scattergraph (empathy versus control). High empathy, low control (e.g., listening, offering choices) fosters trust. High control, low empathy (e.g., demanding compliance) triggers fear. Check your progress weekly: Are you leaning toward empathy? You can have this conversation with older children, "Do you feel like you can trust me?" For younger children, you may opt to use a sheet with various emojis printed on it, asking questions like, "Which of these emojis are you feeling right now? How do I seem when I'm talking to you? Like this (picture) or like this one?"

- **Kinnect challenge**: At home, work with your child to complete a challenge together, for example, building a house with cards or doing a puzzle together for short bursts. Work together, fostering collaboration. This builds connection and peer-like trust, preparing them for school relationships, which is the 1–1 attachment phase of the ARC model. Use LEGO® or Jenga® (or similar activities) as you get more comfortable working together to model good competition, how to fail, and how to win with grace.

PROTECTING YOUR HEART

Advocating in schools is exhausting. Teachers may resist, principals and administrators will push back, and you'll feel the weight of your child's struggles. You'll mess up. It took me a while to learn how to talk to counselors and teachers. I could see things from the kids' lens and that often interfered with my ability to talk about things from the adult and system perspective. But we can learn and continue advocating. Forgive yourself when you falter; you're learning in a system that's often stuck in crisis mode. Protect your heart: rest after tough meetings, journal your frustrations, and seek support from other foster parents or a therapist. Your resilience fuels your child's. You're not just fighting for your child—you're rewriting their school story, one empathetic step at a time.

MOVING FORWARD

School struggles reflect a clash between a child's trauma and a system built for control, not healing. Your advocacy—through ARC, role play, or Kinnect inspired connection—can shift that. Next, we'll explore the runaway impulse, helping kids find safety without fleeing.

Anchoring the Storm– Practical Paths to Trust and Healing

CHAPTER 6

Seeking Safety in Flight–The Runaway Impulse

*R*epeated *trauma in adult life erodes the structure of the personality already formed, but repeated trauma in childhood forms and deforms the personality. The child trapped in an abusive environment is faced with the formidable tasks of adaptation. They must find a way to preserve a sense of trust in adults who are untrustworthy. Safety in a situation that is unsafe, control in a situation that is terrifying, unpredictable power in a situation of helplessness. Unable to care for or protect herself, she must compensate for the failures of adult care and protection with the only means at her disposal—an immature system of psychological defenses.*

–Judith Herman, *Trauma And Recovery*

When a foster kid bolts out the door or clams up in silence, it's easy to feel like you're failing. Their running, whether it's tearing down the street or retreating behind a blank stare, feels personal, like they're rejecting you or your home. But here's the truth: They're not running from you. All too often, an involuntary threat response has been activated by some cue in the environment. They're running from fear, a deep, wired-in instinct that screams "danger" even when they're safe in your living room.

My own childhood taught me this and years of coaching foster kids showed me how to guide that flight toward trust. This chapter weaves together stories, science, and practical tools to help you understand why kids run and how to create safe spaces for them to land. In these stories, we will explore opportunities for connection. When children run, you don't need to chase them—you need to be their anchor.

MY STORY: FLEEING SHAME'S STING

Growing up in my adoptive home, I was always running. Taken from my 18-year-old mother at 2, my brother and I landed with parents whose perception of love was warped into incoherence. By age 15, I'd been through ten schools, each one a fresh battle to fit in.

The summer before tenth grade, we moved again. This time to a rural California town, where I joined the swim team. It was my one place to feel strong, to burn off the energy of a kid who never felt safe. But my adoptive mom, raised to pinch pennies, bought my swim trunks at Goodwill. They were used, of course, and had these random numbers stitched in—315, 475—like some kind of code. At practice, kids pointed and laughed. "What's that?" one of them shouted.

Shame washed over me, hot and heavy. I could've shrunk, but instead, I ran with a lie: "In California, they rank swimmers.

I'm 315th fastest in the 100 freestyle." It was ridiculous, but it was my shield, built from years of dodging rejection. When a teammate's parent called it nonsense, the lie collapsed and I was ashamed all over again.

That shame didn't fade; it fueled a deeper flight, pulling me toward older kids who were out of control—who had cars and access to alcohol. I sought high-tension distractions and risk-taking that drowned out the sting because staying still meant facing the rejection I couldn't escape. It was transference at play: My brain, conditioned to expect shame from adults, projected that onto peers, seeking chaos to avoid vulnerability. I was rejecting connection before it could reject me, building walls of escapism to protect the raw hurt underneath.

Years later, coaching a 13-year-old foster kid, I saw that same flight. He'd skip our sessions, pulling his hoodie low, retreating from the fear of failing me—just as I'd run from the risk of more shame. I didn't push or scold, as he probably expected. Instead, when he did show up, I made sure that I was consistent and predictable in my unconditional regard toward him. We played checkers, Mancala, Connect 4, and Jenga with no pressure, just fun.

Slowly, he stopped running from me. His trust grew with each game, information leaking out a little at a time. That's what you can do—offer a safe place to land rather than a reason to keep fleeing the shame of failure. By recognizing their flight as a defensive strategy, not defiance, you break the cycle by showing them vulnerability can lead to connection, not more pain.

WHY THEY RUN: THE SCIENCE OF FLIGHT

That urge to run (flight) comes from a brain built for survival, not defiance. Imagine a kid's nervous system like a radar, always scanning for danger. Dr. Bruce Perry explains that when a child feels threatened—by a loud voice, a crowded room, or even a memory—their brain kicks into gear instantly, triggering flight in the first ten seconds before they even have time to think.[31] It's like their body is on autopilot, wired to escape harm. Trauma keeps this system on high alert, making kids see threats where you see safety, like your raised eyebrow or a door shut too firmly. Some kids bolt physically, sprinting out the back door, while others run emotionally, shutting down into silence, becoming wallflowers to avoid notice.

Chronic stress from abuse or neglect overloads kids' systems, making it hard for them to pause and plan. Instead of thinking, "I'm safe here," they act on instinct, running to chaos—like risky peers and dark streets—because that's what feels familiar. But here's the hope: Their brains are malleable. With consistent, caring moments, you can help them rewire that instinct, guiding them to seek safety in your presence rather than danger in the world. It's not about stopping their flight— it's about giving them a better place to land.

Think like a coach. Fundamentals and drills are the foundation of mastery, but even before that, a person's internal desire to perform is based on trust and acknowledgment built by predictable, safe interaction. Rigid personalities will become

---

31 Bruce D. Perry and Maia Szalavitz, *The Boy Who Was Raised as a Dog: And Other Stories from a Child Psychiatrist's Notebook—What Traumatized Children Can Teach Us About Loss, Love, and Healing* (New York: Basic Books, 2006), 47.

reactive here, which is taking it personally, and the child becomes the scapegoat again.

WHAT FLIGHT LOOKS LIKE

You might see a 10-year-old dash to the park after you sigh heavily, their brain echoing an abusive past where sighs meant punishment. Or a 12-year-old girl sitting alone on the playground, staring blankly, her silence a shield against rejection. These aren't acts of rebellion, but rather a trauma-built brain seeking safety the only way it knows how.

I have watched too many foster parents and guardians berate their child into sullen submission, retreating in anger, mirroring the emotion of the adult. All too often, the adult seems satisfied that the child isn't lying anymore or being defiant or making excuses for running away. How often have we asked the child why they did it and the answer is "I don't know"? We expect a child to come up with an answer for something that is not well understood even by the most academics and is so individualized, it can only cause bewilderment and shame.

QTIP: Quit Taking It Personally. Their running isn't about you. It's their fear fleeing a threat they can't name. Getting triggered into a survival brain takeover is real. When a trigger occurs, it is our responsibility as caregivers to recognize it and begin to build a coaching plan to replace the fight or flight with a more useful response. I see so many adult survivors who acknowledge their triggers but expect the world to adapt to them. This does not work out well. Remember, you can't know what you don't know but when we do know, we do better.

HOW TO BE THEIR SAFE HAVEN

What Doesn't Work

When a foster kid bolts out the door or sinks into silence, your first instinct might be to take charge and to fix it fast. You chase after them, shouting, "Come back!" or lean in close demanding, "Why won't you talk to me?" It's human to want to stop the chaos, to pull them back to safety. But those reactions, natural as they are, can be like pouring fuel on a wildfire— their fear flares up, burning hotter. Restraining a child who's running tells their trauma-wired brain that you're a threat, not a protector, pushing them to flee further, maybe to a risky street or a dangerous crowd. Scolding a silent kid saying, "You can't just shut down like that," does the same, driving them deeper into isolation, where their mind becomes a fortress you can't reach.

Sometimes we must react because there is a safety issue. Control and restraint may be necessary. However, as quickly as possible in order to interrupt the alienation, shift your attitude and behaviors toward apology and reconciliation with the child. No child wants to be restrained, and we certainly don't want to cause our child to feel fear or fury. Safety requires a proactive plan for what to do in emergencies. That plan needs to be practiced so that you and your child know what to expect and have practiced the execution of that plan. This builds trust and connection even in the midst of a challenging situation once a boundary has been breached.

Foster parents often share similar stories. One mom told me about her 8-year-old foster son who bolted to the backyard every time she corrected his homework. She'd chase him, grabbing his arm to bring him inside, thinking it was discipline. But each time, he ran faster, once climbing a neighbor's fence to escape. Her grip, meant to keep him safe, felt like danger to his trauma-soaked nervous system. There was no proactive plan developed between homework sessions. So, how was he supposed to know what to do other than get better at what he knew—running away?

Another dad described his 14-year-old foster daughter who'd shut down at family dinners and stared at her plate. He'd say, "You're part of this family, talk to us!" But his insistence pushed her further into silence, until she'd get up, go to her room, and lock the door. These reactions—chasing, demanding, restraining—come from care for the child, but to a traumatized kid, they scream threat.

Punishment, like time-outs or taking away privileges, does the same damage. A foster mom once grounded her 11-year-old for running to the park after an argument. He stopped running outside, but then he started hiding under his bed. His flight turned inward, harder to reach.

Consequences feel logical to us, but to a kid whose brain is wired for survival, they're proof that the world is against them. Their fear grows, and so does their need to run: physically to chaos and emotionally to a place you can't follow. The lesson here is hard but true: Trying to control their flight doesn't stop it; it makes them run faster, further, and become even harder to reach.

What Does Work

Instead of chasing them, become a safe haven. For kids who run physically, help them create a "calm corner" in your home. Allow them to select a cozy spot and then help them fill it with things they love, like a blanket, stuffed animal, or a fidget toy. Sit with them during calm times, practicing retreating to this exact spot, saying, "This is your safe place when things feel too big to handle." Practice going there together so when they're triggered, their body knows where to go. If they bolt, don't grab them; walk nearby with a voice soft saying, "I'm here when you're ready."

I have shown up at more than one home where the kid had climbed up a tree as high as they could go. I remember that feeling. Unreachable, safe from my perspective, face turned to the sun and the breeze. Unsafe and terrifying for most adults, but it met the child's need for tension and a sense of control.

For kids who run emotionally, sit close when possible and use a gentle tone: "I'm right here, sweetie. I've got you." Whenever possible, when dealing with a child triggered into flight, sit lower than the child to avoid towering over them. Your calm presence signals safety. Try simple games, like Jenga, letting them feel seen without pressure. A 12-year-old girl I worked with thawed after three games, her blank stare softening as she eventually joined the family for dinner.

Celebrate small wins: If they run to their calm corner twice in ten tries, that's progress. Be curious, like a scientist, noting what triggers their flight—maybe your tone or a loud TV—and adjust your approach.

TOOLS TO GUIDE THEIR FLIGHT

- **Calm corner creation**: With your child, allow them to pick a spot in your home and fill it with comforting items they choose, like a stuffed animal. Practice visiting daily, saying, "This is where we go to feel safe." Within a month of introducing a calming beanbag corner, a 10-year-old I coached stopped running away to the park down the street during moments of overwhelm.
- **Playful connection**: Play Jenga or checkers, saying, "It's okay to take your time." If they freeze, stay calm: "I'm here."
- **Reflect and learn**: Journal: "What sparked their flight today? How can I offer safety?" Example: "He ran after my sigh. I'll soften my voice tomorrow."
- **Build trust**: Commit to one play activity weekly, like kicking a ball, to begin establishing consistency and ritual.
- **Track your calm**: Each day, note your patience versus control. High patience soothes flight; high control fuels it.

HOLDING SPACE FOR YOURSELF

Watching a foster kid run, whether out the door or into silence, can break your heart, stirring a storm of frustration, fear, or even anger. A sense of fear can be common, triggering your own feelings of not being capable. But if we flip it, it is actually an opportunity for you to model how to mend a rift. The practice of self-care in the moment is showing the child "this is how I honor myself"—modeling healthy self-care for children who may not have seen it practiced. And it's in this modeling that you're giving the child permission to begin practicing their own healthy self-care too. This is a core practice when I'm teaching interventions to foster parents and foster youth organizations.

Growing up in a home of chaos, I understand what it's like to carry pain and how quickly it can morph into shame. Coaching foster kids and families has shown me that holding space for them starts with holding space for yourself.

You're human, and you'll stumble. Maybe you snap when a kid bolts, or feel helpless when they shut down. That's okay. Forgive yourself; modeling self-forgiveness is a powerful teaching tool. Those feelings don't make you a bad foster parent; they make you real. It is so much more about what you do rather than what you say. Foster and adoptive kids have been told too many things that weren't true, which creates a brain that is attuned to adult behavior rather than the words they say. Practicing your own stabilization will model and recharge you for the long haul.

Don't go it alone. Lean on a friend, a support group, or a therapist who understands the weight of foster care. Having a supportive local network is something to strive for. Training in PFA (Psychological First Aid) and SPR (Skills for Psychological Recovery) can give you valuable tools for high stress events and ongoing stress management. These are part of the PTSM (Post Traumatic Stress Management) framework of the NCTSN.

Additionally, being trained in the group work of PTSM gives you the opportunity to share in three types of groups: stabilization, satisfaction and self-care. These trainings are available through MTSN (Midwest Trauma Services Network) and ITC (International Trauma Center). You can learn more in the appendix at the end of this book.

Your gentle patience is a child's anchor. When you're steady, you show kids that safety isn't just a place; it's a person. But you can't pour from an empty cup. Rest when you can, even if it's a nap while they're at school. Celebrate your wins, too, like the day a kid runs to their calm corner instead of the street. Those moments matter. You're not just guiding their flight; you're building a bridge to trust and that starts with caring for *yourself*.

THE PATH AHEAD

Flight is a foster kid's brain, wired by trauma to run from fear, seeking safety. It's not defiance; it's survival, a reflex carved by pain. But you have the power to change that path. Your steady presence, playful connection, and safe spaces, like a calm corner or a game of Jenga, guide them to trust one small moment at a time. Progress won't be fast or tidy. Some days, they'll still bolt or shut down, and you'll wonder if you're enough. You are. Each time you stay calm, offer play, or sit quietly nearby, you're rewiring their brain and teaching them safety is here with you.

This journey doesn't end with flight. Next, in chapter 7, we'll dive into the fight impulse when kids yell, hit, or hurt themselves, battling a world they see as unsafe. Just as you guide their running, you can shape their aggression into connection, helping them feel seen without fighting the world or themselves. Your patience and love are the threads weaving flight and fight into healing, showing kids they're worth staying for and worth fighting for.

CHAPTER 7

Fighting to Survive– Aggression and Control

When a foster kid lashes out—yelling, breaking things, or hurting themselves—it hits you like a storm. Their aggression, whether it's a meltdown over a lost game or hidden scars, feels like a rejection of your care, a sign that you're failing. But here's a truth I've carried from my own battles: It's not about you. It's a trauma-wired brain fighting to survive, seeing threats in every sharp word or sidelong glance.

I grew up fighting to be seen, and coaching foster kids taught me how to guide that fight toward trust. This chapter weaves stories, science, and tools to help you understand the fight impulse, channel it into safe expression, and turn battles into bridges for connection. You don't need to control their anger; you need to show them that it's safe to feel it with you.

MY STORY: FIGHTING TO FIND MY PLACE

In my adoptive home, the air was thick with unspoken rules and simmering tension. I learned to fight early not only with words that cut like knives, but also with fists that bruised both body and soul. Aggression became my shield, the tool handed to me to survive in a world that felt perpetually unsafe, where love was conditional and vulnerability was seen as a weakness. But no matter how fiercely I swung, nearly every fight ended in tears and anguish. It never brought the peace I so desperately craved. Instead, it left me feeling hollow, chasing shadows of control in a home that offered none.

I'd comply on the surface, nodding along when my adoptive parents were within earshot or eyesight, but the instant their gaze shifted, I'd probe every limit like a caged animal testing the bars. By fourth grade, I was already lacing up gloves at the local boys' club, pounding out my frustrations on punching bags and opponents.

My adoptive father, perhaps seeing his own unresolved pains in me, gave advice that echoed his worldview: at my new school, find the biggest kid and punch him square in the mouth to carve out your spot in the pecking order. I didn't question it. I followed through, blood on my knuckles and a twisted sense of pride in meeting his expectations. But each brawl, each scrape in the schoolyard, deepened the scar on my heart. Fights weren't just physical—they were affirmations of the label I carried: bad kid. The stares from classmates, the whispers from teachers, and the wary distance from potential friends all reinforced that belief, making it harder to see any other path.

What I couldn't grasp then was the conditioning at play—a subtle wiring from years of chaos and rejection. My actions weren't born from innate evil but from a brain shaped by survival, reacting to threats both real and perceived. For many foster kids today, it's much the same. Aggression isn't defiance for its own sake. It's a desperate bid to feel powerful in a world that's stripped away their control. As foster parents, recognizing this cycle—breaking it with patience, consistency, and understanding—can rewrite that story, turning fighters into kids who finally feel safe enough to lower their guards.

But that's not enough! It is one thing to establish safety, but if we don't teach other skills, the earlier conditioning will fight its way through the safety and begin to slowly move the things back to what they are comfortable with not because they want to or are even conscious of it, but because it satisfies their need for the familiar chaos and tension.

I was consulting in a juvenile detention unit for a respected agency in the Midwest after the massive shifts that occurred after the 2018 Federal Families First legislation. This detention center had lost most of its senior leadership and expertise due to budget cuts. There was an expectation that the quality of the unit should remain the same without the benefit of the robust and dense leadership scaffolding that had existed before. To be fair, there were still great leaders in this organization, but they were overwhelmed—each one doing the work of three people now that staffing was reduced.

When the 2016 Families First legislation was introduced, I was working for a Native tribe in Washington State. I was asked by their child welfare department to do a presentation for their MOU (Memorandum of Understanding) meeting with the state. It attracted a large variety of human services workers, including a regional director at the federal level. That person introduced themselves to me before the program began and asked to have lunch after the morning presentation.

In my presentation, I went into the dynamics of child welfare as I saw them. I talked about the Families First legislation and how the shifts would fail because they would not be funded to be successful. There would not be enough training, staffing, or reimbursement. The regional director walked out of the presentation, and I never saw them again. I had to find a new lunch meeting that day. They took it personally. It was a system issue, and they chose to avoid the difficult but necessary conversation.

As a consultant for child welfare across the country, I would do unit observations at local juvenile facilities, watching and contributing as I could. In one location, the staff were managing nine kids who were involved with the Juvenile Justice system and clearly some of them needed mental health support too. Watching the clients amuse themselves by sophisticated and subtle manipulation of the staff was amazing to witness. And because resources were limited, the unit felt like a fishbowl most of the time. No escape. So, the unit operated in subtle chaos constantly. The staff were doing the best they could, and the clients were becoming more adept at antisocial subversion, getting better at what they were already good at.

Almost all kids who have grown up in intense environments need to satisfy their tension. If we don't give them prosocial outlets, they will adapt on their own through the antisocial, egocentric behavior they are masterful in. To get a kid to do a new behavior, safety, consistency, predictability, and unconditional regard have to happen long enough for basic trust to exist—and that trust allows vulnerability to grow.

WHY THEY FIGHT: THE SCIENCE OF AGGRESSION

Aggression isn't defiance—it's a brain wired to survive. Picture a foster kid's nervous system like a volcano, ready to erupt at the smallest tremor. When a child feels threatened, whether by a raised voice or a memory, their brain shifts into survival mode and triggers a fight response, literally in a millisecond, before they can think. It's their body acting on fear, not reason. Trauma keeps this volcano simmering, causing kids to read your frown as danger, sparking yells, destruction, or self-harm. For some, the struggle turns outward—breaking things or shouting. For others, it turns inward through things like pulling their own hair or self-harm (cutting) to feel control.

Chronic stress floods their system with cortisol, fueling aggression and disrupting calm. Trauma weakens their ability to pause, so fear drives action. But their brains can change. With consistent, safe moments, you can help them channel anger into healthy expression—like hitting a pillow or drawing their feelings—rewiring the fight into trust. It's about guiding their energy, not crushing it.

WHAT FIGHTING LOOKS LIKE

Fighting might be an 11-year-old girl screaming insults after a foster sibling's tease, her words a shield against rejection. Or a 14-year-old boy banging his fists on a desk at school, his frustration echoing past failures. I worked with a teenager who would bang her head violently on the floor when overwhelmed, her pain a desperate grasp for control. These aren't attacks—they are traumas plea for safety. **QTIP: Quit Taking It Personally**. Their aggression is fear battling a threat for which there are no words. How can they explain something to someone when they have no vocabulary for it?

HOW TO SHAPE THEIR FIGHT

What Doesn't Work

When a foster kid yells, breaks something, or hurts themselves, your instinct is to shut it down and restore peace. You shout, "Stop it!" or send them to their room, hoping consequences teach control. But those reactions, born of love and exhaustion, are like tossing fuel on a fire; their fear blazes hotter, pushing them to fight more fiercely. Yelling at a tantrum or restraining a kid who's lashing out tells their trauma-wired brain you're a threat—not a safe haven—driving them to swing harder or turn their pain inward. Punishing for self-harm, like grounding or taking privileges, deepens their belief that pain is their only power.

Many times I have been caught off guard, resulting in a reactive response from a child. On one occasion, I remarked on some new snow boots that a young lady had on. As my work partner and I came into the shelter that she was housed in, she snapped at me, "They're not new!"

She suddenly spun away from me and sat down with a thump on the steps of the home. I apologized and sat down on a step lower than hers, on the other side of the steps. I then started talking to my work partner about the visit. After a moment, my partner nodded her head toward the 10-year-old, and I turned to look at the girl. She was sliding a piece of candy across the step toward me but still looking away from me. How amazing is that! I didn't take her rebuke personally; I apologized and normalized, and she quickly settled and reconnected in the only way she knew how. **QTIP: Quit Taking It Personally**.

Foster parents know this struggle. We consulted on a case in which a 9-year-old boy was about to be put on antipsychotics because when he was triggered, he would start screaming about blood in the air. He would get really violent and unapproachable. As we got to know him and heard a little of his story, some details came out that we were able to corroborate in his file that explained both his words and his fear. Once we were able to help the family understand that it was a traumatic reenactment, they were able to respond differently and the episodes stopped almost immediately.

Punishment feels right, but it can fuel chaos. Consequences like time-outs or lost privileges tell kids their anger is wrong, not safe to feel. Their fear grows, and so does their fight, outward to destruction or inward to pain. The truth is hard. Too often, controlling their aggression doesn't teach control; it teaches them to fight harder, further from trust.

What Does Work

Your job is to redirect their anger, like guiding a river to a new path. For kids with outward aggression, introduce a "fight pillow," a sturdy cushion specifically for hitting that is different from the pillows you sleep with. Practice during calm moments: "This is for big feelings. Try a punch." If they yell, stay steady: "I'm here. Let's try the pillow."

This is not an end point. This is simply the beginning of shaping a behavior into something more healthy and less dangerous. The feelings get out, and no one gets hurt.

Play builds trust. Whether they are drumming or drawing, kids feel seen. Drumming sessions—rhythm—build focus and teach children how to use their energy. The number of times I have been in a family's backyard and ended up in a contest to see who could throw balls (or walnuts or rocks) into a bucket is too many to remember. And it often turned into a ritual each time I visited that home.

Be curious, noting triggers like when a sibling teases, so you can be prepared to intervene and calm fears. Celebrate wins: Two pillow hits in ten tries is growth. Model repair: If you snap, say, "I'm sorry. Let's try again." In a group activity, I used peacock feathers for kids to balance, teaching focus. An angry girl mastered it, her pride replacing shouts. These moments show anger can shift to connection with you as their guide.

TOOLS TO CHANNEL THEIR FIGHT

- **Fight pillow practice**: Introduce a pillow for hitting. Practice daily: "This is for big feelings."
- **Playful connection**: Play drumming or drawing, saying, "It's okay to mess up." Redirect fights to the pillow.
- **Reflect and learn**: Journal: "What sparked their fight? How can I guide it?" Example: "She yelled after another

child teased her. I'll watch how she responds to sibling dynamics."

- **Build trust**: Commit to one weekly play activity, like drawing.
- **Track your calm**: Note patience versus control daily. High patience soothes; high control escalates.
- **Rainbowdance**: For preschool and elementary ages, use rhythm games like Rainbowdance. See appendix for more information.

HOLDING SPACE FOR YOURSELF

Facing a foster kid's aggression, whether yelling, breaking things, or self-harm, can leave you raw. It stirs frustration, fear, and even anger, which can weigh you down. I still feel those same emotions when a kid goes off because of some unseen cue. That moment echoed my childhood—fighting or fleeing in a home of chaos, my father's PTSD, my mother's struggles— where I learned to carry pain alone. Coaching taught me that holding space for kids starts with holding space for yourself.

You're human, and you'll stumble. Maybe you snap when a kid yells, or feel helpless when they hurt themselves. That's okay. Forgive yourself. Those feelings don't make you less; they make you real. A foster dad I worked with felt crushed after his 14-year-old's desk banging at school. He blamed himself, but after some psychoeducation about development and trauma, he stopped taking it personally and used his most familiar coping skills. He started sketching his frustrations, finding calm in his pen and ink drawings. Another foster mom felt drained after her 10-year-old broke toys. She took evening walks, breathing deep, letting tension fade. Small acts, like sketching, walking, or having a quiet cup of tea—whatever brings you back to the present—will recharge you for the journey.

Don't face it alone! We humans were meant to raise children in a large family context. Lean on a friend, a foster care group, or a therapist who understands the weight. My experiences as a Navy Diver, a dolphin handler, and my work with the Tulalip Tribes showed me a community's power. They taught me to pause, breathe, and stay steady in chaos.

You need that circle to lift you. A foster parent joined a group, sharing fears about her 8-year-old's meltdowns. Hearing stories from others, she felt stronger and less alone. Your calm is their anchor, but you can't give from an empty well. Rest. Find your way to peace in little moments: singing a hymn or playing an instrument, practicing Tai Chi on YouTube, walking with a neighbor, or discovering connection, rhythm, and laughter. You deserve peace.

Celebrate your wins, like when a kid chooses a pillow over a wall. You're not just guiding their fight; you're building trust, shaping change, and that starts with caring for yourself.

THE PATH AHEAD

Fighting is a foster kid's brain seeking control, wired by trauma to battle fear. It's not rebellion; it's survival, a reflex born of pain. But your steady presence, playful connection, and safe spaces, like a fight pillow or drumming session, guide them to trust, one moment at a time. Progress will be slow and messy. Some days, they'll yell or hurt you, and you'll doubt yourself.

You're enough. Each time you stay calm, offer play, or sit quietly nearby, you rewire their brain, showing safety is here with you.

This journey continues beyond fighting. In chapter 8, we'll tackle medical triggers—when doctor visits or misdiagnoses spark fear or aggression.

Discipline With Love—Shaping Behavior With Care

Disciplining a foster kid is like navigating a stormy sea. Their defiance, like slamming doors or ignoring rules, can make you want to yell or ground them. But punishment often sparks fear rather than trust. In a trauma-wired brain, rules mean, "I don't have control. Someone else is controlling me." Let me be clear: Boundaries and consequences are more important for trauma kids than they are for kids in good enough homes; they just don't believe the rules are real. I've coached kids who tested every limit, and I've learned that discipline is about showing safety through consistent, loving boundaries. You don't need to control them in order to help them learn healthy self-discipline. You need to be their steady drumbeat; their safe place.

MY STORY: LEARNING BOUNDARIES

Because of the lack of consistency in my childhood, the constant terror at home and frequently moving to new areas,

I was impulsive and reactive, seeking adult input through judgment and punishment. It was all I knew. Even when boundaries *were* set, I didn't believe them. They had never been consistent and reliable before and to believe them would mean being let down again. Why would I expect that now? Remember that scene in one of the *Jurassic Park* movies where the predator dinosaurs constantly test the electrified barriers that surround their cage? Yeah, exactly.

So, every new set of teachers and coaches in a new town dealt with my impulsive, reactive behaviors. I had no expectation of a good interaction with an adult, and when a good experience *did* occur, I couldn't afford to receive them emotionally with grace. I couldn't afford to trust this adult. My conditioning wouldn't allow me to be vulnerable to have a good experience with an adult. I couldn't override my defensiveness, not even to *try*.

Those kinds of interactions were the oddity, not the norm. I didn't know how to handle them because I didn't have enough practice. I was an expert at the negative interactions. But a nice, pleasant adult who was genuinely interested in me? That was weird.

Then, in the summer before my sophomore year in high school, I found a swim coach who consistently expressed "unconditional regard" toward my teammates and me. He never reacted to my behavior in a negative way, even though I was constantly challenging the culture of the team. He set the tone not only for the coaching staff, but for the parent group as well. Sure, on a swim team with 120 parents, you would expect to have some outspoken adults who didn't approve of me, but many other parents followed his lead and were supportive and unconditional in the way they interacted with me.

This created a consistent culture that I slowly gravitated toward over the next few years. I allowed myself to get comfortable there, to practice working inside boundaries, becoming more disciplined in the context of that sport I loved.

Three things made this a pivotal, significant transitional time for me. It's probably why I ended up in the military—and not in prison.

1. The challenge of learning to live within Coach's boundaries and the physical exertion of swimming daily redirected some of my natural energy.
2. Having this large group of adults and their kids (my teammates) who esteemed me in spite of my impulsive, rebellious behaviors showed me that I *could be* esteemed. I won the award for best swimmer and diver my sophomore year, which was affirming but also challenged my emotional maturity.
3. We lived there for the last three years of my high school career. I finally found some stability in my peer group.

WHY DISCIPLINE CHALLENGES THEM

Trauma shapes a foster kid's brain to expect danger, not structure. Foster kids' high rates of mental health challenges, like anxiety or oppositional behavior, stem from abuse or neglect, making rules feel like threats.[32] Harsh discipline

---

32 Amy D. Engler et al., "A Systematic Review of Mental Health Disorders of Children in Foster Care," *Trauma, Violence, & Abuse* 23, no. 1 (2022): 255–64, https://doi.org/10.1177/1524838020941197

worsens emotional regulation in foster kids who lack secure attachment to trust consistent limits. Trauma disrupts their ability to process long term consequences, so grounding feels like rejection.[33]

Kids learn good, healthy boundaries from love, not fear. When their nervous systems are wired by chaos, they crave predictability, but it makes them too uncomfortable. With short, trauma-informed boundaries, you can rewire their brains for safety. But it takes time, consistency, and predictability.

WHAT DISCIPLINE CHALLENGES LOOK LIKE

When discipline means taking things away from foster kids, it often backfires, especially without having already established a foundation of trust. Picture a child who's taken something that's not theirs and is hiding it in their room. You find it and, as a consequence, take their belongings to "teach them a lesson." Their response? Anger erupts. They throw or break their things, maybe even shout, "Take it all!" This isn't just defiance; it's their way of showing that material possessions can't control them. Some might think, "Let them go without for a few days." But for kids without secure attachment, solid self-esteem, or empathy, this approach is a trap.

For foster kids shaped by trauma, the world often feels like a place where worth is tied to "things" like what you own or how you look, rather than who you are. When you take their

---

33 Bruce D. Perry and Maia Szalavitz, *The Boy Who Was Raised as a Dog: And Other Stories from a Child Psychiatrist's Notebook—What Traumatized Children Can Teach Us About Loss, Love, and Healing* (New York: Basic Books, 2006), 112.

possessions as punishment, you're not just removing objects—you're stripping away a fragile anchor they've clung to in a life of instability.

Without the foundation of trust, intimacy, or vulnerability, this new loss pushes them toward a cold, perhaps even institutional, mindset where survival means shutting down emotionally. I've seen kids empty their rooms, smashing toys or tossing clothes, not out of spite, but as a desperate declaration: "You can't break me this way." Their resentment, resistance, or even revenge isn't hatred; it's fear, a cry from a heart that's known too much loss. Instead of taking it personally, pause and recognize their reaction as a plea for connection. Building that bond with patience and presence, rather than stripping away their sense of security, is what paves the way for healing.

Valuing material possessions is just a stepping stone toward the greater goal of high self-worth. It is superficial, and it will never be enough because it can't fill the void of not being loved or valued as a human being. The more care that can be demonstrated for the individual, the more a young person can step into and master vulnerability, which then leads to intimacy and deeper co-regulation, which means being in tune with other people in peace and safety.

The other side of this is that using material possessions as rewards or punishments for a child who is missing the core needs of attachment and esteem overemphasizes those things in the context of adult life. When a kid is punished by withholding material possessions, quite often they learn that material possessions mean something to other people and become a way for those children to punish society when they grow up. Acts of vandalism or property theft, especially if it's to fund their stunted coping skills, are also interwoven with a thread of "getting even" running through their immature social justice view.

HOW TO SHAPE BEHAVIOR

What Doesn't Work

The number of times I have heard "That kid just needs to be taken out back and have his ass beat" is far too high. Here's the simple truth: This "kid" has likely already had his "butt beat" many times. If it hasn't worked yet, why would it work now? What will likely happen if that kid gets humiliated or "beaten" is that many other people downstream will pay the price for it.

Many other innocent people will suffer because this child—who doesn't understand empathy, self-esteem, and prosocial attachment—learned that when people make you angry, you beat them up. That's what they have been taught. Now project that attitude into adulthood and look around you. What are we teaching?

Herein lies a glimpse into how foster care and its associated trauma and toxic stress fuel a pipeline directly toward prison, especially for boys. Even more so for minority boys.

When a kid defies you—throwing toys, skipping curfew—your instinct is to take charge. You shout, "Stop!" or ground them for weeks believing it sets limits. But those reactions, born of frustration, are like sparks on dry grass. Their trauma reads your anger as danger, fueling defiance or withdrawal. The "go-to" punishment response of many parents, yelling or long punishments, has been shown to deepen mistrust.[34] Yelling, long consequences, or reactive rules tell kids boundaries mean control, not care.

What Does Work

Part of your job is coaching: setting short, clear boundaries with love. Try using short 15-minute consequences: "No screens until dinner, then we'll play", rather than "A week without screens!"

I coached a 13-year-old who slammed doors when he got angry; a 30-minute "cool-down" with a stress ball, followed by a game of catch, eased his anger. Play 1 on 1 games, like Connect Four, setting clear rules: "When I lose, I say 'good game.'" Play-based coaching teaches self-regulation in a safe, nonthreatening manner.

I once observed a first grader who was isolated outside and played alone. When I went outside to be around him, he was engaged in aggressive play and language, pounding the dirt and yelling, lost in his trauma reenactment. I watched for a couple of minutes, then walked over to a ball that was laying in the grass and kicked it to him. He ignored it for a couple of seconds, then got up and kicked the ball in the other direction, away from me.

I remarked "Nice kick!" Then I went over to the ball and kicked it to him again. He began to come back from where he was internally, and we ended up having a nice little playtime, which

---

34 Knotts Family Agency, "Improving Foster Care: Best Practices for Agencies," *Knotts Family Agency*, accessed December 10, 2025, https://knottsfamilyagency.org/agency-best-practices/

led to good interactions over the school year. I didn't take it personally when he kicked the ball the other way, and that opened the door to a way for him to connect.

Be curious about triggers, including your tone. Repair mistakes as quickly as you can: "I'm sorry I yelled. Let's try again." Celebrate wins—one "good game" is progress. Consistency makes boundaries feel safe. These moments over time turn tests into trust.

TOOLS TO SHAPE BEHAVIOR

- **Short consequences**: Use shorter limits. "No screens until dinner."
- **Playful coaching**: Play two-player games like Connect Four or Jenga.
- **Reflect and learn**: Journal: "What sparked defiance? How can I guide?" Example: "She yelled when I said 'no.' I'll try a different tactic tomorrow."
- **Build trust**: Commit to one weekly play activity, like catch.
- **Track your calm**: Note when you're responding in patience versus when you're responding reactively. Patience guides; reaction pushes away.
- **Model repair**: Apologize. "I'm sorry, let's restart."

HOLDING SPACE FOR YOURSELF

Defiance can wear you down like waves eroding a shoreline. Picture a beautiful home on a cliff overlooking the ocean. The big storm comes, which you were not prepared for. The cliff erodes, and your home slides into destruction. While this is a stark metaphor, it is also indicative of the way that an overwhelmed foster care system brings the storm to your house and drops it off—hungry, dirty, and with only a few worldly possessions.

Know your limits and set good boundaries, but know also that a life worth living is the gratitude and elation that comes with stretching your boundaries.

Oh yes, you'll stumble. Maybe you yell at defiance or feel lost when rules fail. Forgive yourself—you're human. I have seen so many foster parents on the verge of tears because they feel alone. Trauma does that—it sneaks in and makes you feel less than perfect. It makes you wary of telling other people what's really going on. You may wear a brave face, but you're not feeling safe. Small acts—like journaling, walking, a quiet cup of tea—recharge you and are excellent ways to model self-care for the kids.

THE PATH AHEAD

Discipline for foster kids is about teaching trust through loving boundaries. Their tests are trauma's cry for safety. Your steady presence and playful coaching repair and rewire their brains, which shows that limits mean care. Progress is slow. Some days they'll defy, and you'll doubt. You're enough. Each calm rule or game builds trust.

Next, in chapter 9, we'll explore building bonds—how your modeling and play foster healthy relationships. We'll share stories, like a boy learning to trust through games, and tools to connect, helping kids feel safe. Your love shapes their future.

CHAPTER 9

Building Bonds—Modeling Healthy Relationships

Building a bond with a foster kid is like tending to a fragile rosebush. It needs steady care, patience, and showing up. Their tests, like clinging, lying, or shutting down, can feel like rejection, but they're actually reaching out for trust, shaped by a past where love came with strings. Your actions—your calm, playful tone—will teach them what healthy relationships look like. This chapter blends stories, science, and tools to model connection through authenticity, turning fear into trust. You don't need perfection; you just need to show up.

MY STORY: FINDING CONNECTION

Once I knew that I was adopted, I rejected the idea that *this* was my family. I felt the certainty of this rejection at such a deep level that I could not describe, but it played out in my behavior each time I was berated or shamed. My head would rise, and I would look down my nose at my mom. This would send her over the edge, a tirade of rejection that culminated in her nickname for me: "The Big It." She would mock and berate me, saying things like, "You think you are the *Big It*."

Where did it come from? Why did I behave that way, and what emboldened that behavior? When I eventually met my birth family it became clear. I had been highly esteemed as a toddler by my extended family. My aunties and uncles spoke of carrying me around on their hips. Unfortunately, I don't have any actual memories of this, but clearly it was in my emotional memory. It would emerge as almost a haughtiness when I was berated by my adoptive parents.

At 32 years old, I met my birth family, and my grandmother insisted I come live with her. I thought, *whoa, I don't even know you!* The thought of living with someone I didn't know made me feel awkward and uncomfortable. People were telling me that I had to live with her and my instinctive response was immediately to reject that. Who did these people think they were? I didn't have to listen to them. I had felt in control of my own environment for 16 years by this point. I had no desire to allow anyone else to have that weight or authority over me again.

It was not long before my aunts and uncles were ganging up on me. They explained the family structure, where I fit in, and that it was my duty as the "oldest" to do as my grandmother said. These people I didn't know were suddenly telling me what I was going to do! Certainly not!

And yet, I also had an irresistible desire to know this family, explore these relationships, and learn more about myself and my heritage. Within six weeks, I was living with my biological grandmother.

For the first time in my life, I experienced unconditional love and nurturing. I could do no wrong! She cooked for me and cared for me as if I were precious and important to her! She told me family stories and made me feel connected to the previous generations in ways I could never have imagined. This had a profound impact on my understanding of what life could be. It was an important step toward understanding that there were things I didn't know yet.

Over the years, many teachers said something along the lines of, "I don't get it. You have so much potential." They had no words for the way I had learned to mask my vulnerability. Of course, I could not explain it either. It was only when I found something that I was good at, something that only I could excel at, that I began to gravitate toward and ultimately benefit from the constant esteem in that area of my life.

A child in trauma can't afford to accept feeling good about something because that makes them vulnerable to being hurt by that very thing. Remember in chapter 8 when we talked about possessions and the futility of taking toys away? The subliminal message that children with high trauma histories receive is that if they begin to feel attached to something (whether a possession, a person, or an activity), they are now at risk of getting hurt by the removal or the loss of that very thing. And so this often triggers the child to lash out first: to break the toy, to damage the relationship, to quit the activity, or to rebel against it.

It's an instinctive protective response rather than a conscious decision. It takes time and trust for the child's internal protective mechanism to change that instinctive response.

The only place I ever really felt like I belonged, before I met my birth family, was in the swimming pool. I loved getting in the pool and swimming hard. I joined teams in many of the areas where we lived. It became a familiar connection that I could carry with me to each new school and community. I enjoyed the effort it required, strengthening my muscles. And my hard work paid off in some small successes, which fueled my competitive nature.

I had several excellent head coaches, and many of my teammates' parents approved and encouraged my effort and capability. Over time, this translated into a basic sense of belonging. I had a lot of acquaintances on the swim team. Not really friends, but we were around each other a lot.

And, as part of these teams, I got invited into WONDEROUS houses that were so different from mine. I remember a prominent family inviting me over for dinner several times, although I was not the same age as their kids. They understood and gave me access to adults who had successfully gotten through tough times and done well for themselves. This gave me a template of connection, even though I didn't understand it at the time.

I was a good swimmer but not a very good teammate; I was still very much using "an immature set of psychological defenses." Swimming set the stage for me to later become a Navy Diver. And in Combat Dive School, I had an opportunity to work with Force Recon Marines. We spent two months together learning and enduring the challenges.

I was not a good runner and when we would do our long beach runs, I would lose cadence and throw up three or four times during a 12-mile run. We ran in formation and, after a couple of runs, the Marines put their largest Marine behind me. When I would lose cadence, he would put his hand on my back to keep me in rhythm.

In much the same way, because I was a strong swimmer, the Marine officer assigned the weakest swimmer for me to support. On our long ocean swims, I would grab his horse collar and pull him along at a higher speed, connecting through hard work. That experience resonated in my physiology in a very powerful way, though I had yet to understand it rationally.

It became the foundation for the way I look at helping hurting kids gain their footing. I can't stress enough how important it is to do hard things with other people. It is the solution!

WHY RELATIONSHIPS ARE HARD

Trauma robs foster kids of a blueprint for trust. Neglect or abuse disrupts attachment, making kids hyper-alert to your tone or posture, expecting betrayal. Foster kids define family through mutual care but struggle to trust new bonds due to past rejection.[35] Foster youth crave relationships with adults who listen and model respect, yet they fear abandonment. Play builds bonds. These moments show kids that trust is real with

---

35 Annemiek Steenbakkers et al., "Foster Children's Views of Family: A Systematic Review and Qualitative Synthesis," *Children and Youth Services Review* 121 (2021): Article 105879, https://doi.org/10.1016/j.childyouth.2020.105879.

you as their model. Until a trusting relationship is established, being exposed to external control teaches fear; love teaches trust. Your job is to model trust like a coach.

Their brain, wired by chaos, seeks safety. With time and consistency, your calm presence and playful connection reshape their ability to trust.

HOLDING SPACE FOR YOURSELF

Tests against your patience and your boundaries can fray you, like a rope under strain. Their pushback sparks doubt or hurt. I felt it when a 12-year-old's silence triggered my frustration, and my curt tone hurt their trust. I apologized, breathed deeply, and stayed steady. Coaching taught me that you can't model trust if you're not grounded.

You'll falter—maybe you scold a lie or pull away from a clinging child. Forgive yourself; you're human. A foster mom felt drained after her 14-year-old's lies. We had a psychoeducation session about the child's life experience and the meaning of the lies. She journaled nightly, finding peace in the release of emotions, tension, and the weight of not feeling good enough to care for this child. Taking care of yourself doesn't have to happen in big, grandiose ways. Consistency is far more important.

THE PATH AHEAD

Building bonds with foster kids isn't about grand gestures or flawless parenting. It's the quiet power of showing up, day after day, with play, calm, and honest repairs. Their tests aren't rejections; they're trauma's raw plea for safety—a hand reaching out in the dark. Your steady presence—a soft "I'm here" when someone makes a misstep or your laugh instead of frustration over a fallen Jenga tower—rewires their brain.

These small interactions, seemingly inconsequential in the moment, whisper that relationships can be safe instead of stormy. It's slow work, messy and unpredictable. Some days, they'll push you away, hide behind silence, or lash out, and you'll doubt if you are making a dent. But you are enough. Every game you play, every soft word you offer, every time you model repair with a simple "I'm sorry, let's try again," you're carving a path from fear to trust, one small, brave moment at a time.

This isn't just about peace in your home; it's the ripple that changes lives. Keep going, even when it's hard. As Maya Angelou said, "When we knew better, we did better." You're doing better every day, and so are they.

Next, in chapter 10, we'll tackle the challenges of a new arrival—their guarded eyes, silent stares, and the "honeymoon phase" that's more about survival than peace. We'll dive into psychological first aid, sharing stories and tools to make those first days a true welcome, helping your foster kid feel like they can be themselves.

Welcoming With Safety— Psychological First Aid for New Foster Kids

When a foster kid steps into your home, they have likely just endured a very fearful transition and are scared, guarded, and hyperalert. That "honeymoon phase" where they're overly polite or quiet? It's not calm; it's survival. I've worked with many children who arrived with all of their belongings in garbage bags—their world upended.

The first few days are a prime opportunity for you to build trust and show safety rather than rules. PFA (see appendix for more information) gives you a map to meet their needs without judgment, building trust quickly. Just like an emergency room nurse triages emergencies, you will learn to triage trust and safety through the stories, science, and tools in this chapter for each new child who enters your home. Those early moments can become a safe harbor, setting the stage for connection.

MY STORY: FINDING SAFETY

From toddlerhood to tenth grade, my life was a revolving door of new houses, new schools, new everything. Each year brought unfamiliar hallways and another set of faces I would soon call friends, if only for a short time. I was always starting over, never settling, never building on what came before. My connections formed in the rush of new beginnings but without the anchor of lasting relationships, they frayed quickly. This relentless cycle of "new" stretched beyond people to the shifting rules of teachers, dress codes, and the ever-changing pulse of each community I landed in.

For a foster kid, this chaos wasn't just disruption. It was a survival test, forcing me to adapt quickly to each new environment and friend group without the safety of stability. Each move carved a deeper longing for something steady and a place where I could belong without always starting from scratch.

Because of my conditioning, I was fully into risk taking by the end of sixth grade. The summer before seventh grade, I was at a friend's house down the street, high up in a tree. I fell out and broke my arm so severely that I needed a body cast to immobilize the whole arm.

When my friend ran to my house to tell my dad what happened, he told me to walk home. So the ambulance showed up, and the next morning I woke up in a full torso cast…which proceeded to break almost weekly. Why? Because I was still wetting the bed at that age (anxiety based), it was soaking into my cast, and

I smelled like urine at school. So I found ways to break my cast and get a new one.

While there was a lot of shame and emotional abuse around this, it actually extended the lack of control of bodily functions during late adolescence. I now understand much more about somatic complaints and symptoms than many other trauma experts. (You can learn more about this by studying Polyvagal literature, especially the work of Sue Carter and Stephen Porges).

On the final day I had my body cast, I was playing tag with some other kids at the local Boys Club, running away as fast as I could. I got tagged from behind, knocking me off balance. My hard shell cast hit the linoleum tile floor. I turned into a sled that only stopped when I hit the Coke machine at the end of the hallway, shattering the cast once again.

At the doctor's office, my doctor said "Well, it was coming off that day anyway," and then he proceeded to berate me, saying I was "killing my mother" with shame. But what about what she was doing to me?

As the cast came off, the doctor inspected my arm, swore under his breath and had me x-rayed. I had broken my wrist in the Coke machine crash and left his office in a forearm cast for another six weeks. New school, new house, new developmental phase, bigger, faster body, higher tolerance for risk.

WHY NEW ARRIVALS ARE HARD

A foster kid's brain, wired by trauma, sees new homes as threats. Judith Herman writes, "Unable to care for or protect herself, she must compensate for the failures of adult care and protection with the only means at her disposal, an immature system of psychological defenses."[36] Foster kids' anxiety spikes in new settings, driving either compliance or defiance as a survival response. Their nervous systems crave predictability, but chaos taught them to expect betrayal. Kids need safety first in order to trust later.

How do you build trust? You're an 8- or 12- or 14-year-old, and you're expected to simply "build trust" for the very first time? And add to that, you're expected to build it with virtual strangers. That's like asking a kid who's never learned to swim to dive into the deep end and trust the water won't swallow them whole. It's overwhelming and scary, and their brain screams, "No way! This could end badly, just like before."

Developmentally specific secure attachment coaching is the gentle hand that helps them wade in slowly, building a foundation of trust one step at a time (see appendix for more information). This isn't a one-size-fits-all fix; it's tailored to their age and experiences. For an 8-year-old, it might mean short, playful rituals like a daily high-five or choosing a bedtime story—showing consistency without pressure. A 12-year-old might need space to share one positive thing about their day, easing into vulnerability. By 14, it could involve role playing tough conversations, like asking for help without fear of rejection. These steps honor where they are as they learn the basics of safety while guiding them toward deeper connection.

---

36 Judith L. Herman, *Trauma and Recovery* (New York: Basic Books, 1992), 96.

Kids need to know safety first so they can use that as a bridge to learn to trust. It's a process, far slower than you or I may want, but rushing it only reinforces their fear that adults can't be counted on. Their hyperalert brain scans for danger: your tone, your rules, even the way you shift in your chair.

Focusing on safety and comfort rewires their expectation of care, turning "strangers" into "safe people" one small, steady moment at a time. I saw this with a 10-year-old boy I coached who arrived silent and guarded, expecting punishment for every question. We started with simple choices: "This blanket or this other one?" By week three, he was sharing his favorite color. That's the power of developmentally specific coaching: It meets them where they are, building trust brick by brick, until they can dive in without fear.

WHAT NEW ARRIVALS LOOK LIKE

A new kid might be a 6-year-old boy, silent, clutching a toy, fearing it'll be taken. Or a 14-year-old girl, overly polite, masking her fear of rejection. I coached an 11-year-old who asked for snacks nonstop. His bottomless appetite needed to know that his days of hunger were truly over. These aren't manipulations; they're trauma's plea. **QTIP: Quit Taking It Personally**. They're operating from survival, not defiance.

Enjoy the honeymoon period while you can. It's a brief respite for your child where they often adopt an overly compliant demeanor, trying to be your "best kid ever." Eventually, the weight of the mask becomes too heavy, cracks begin to show, and they cannot maintain it. Their "real" self starts to emerge. They're often fearful about how you will react to their "true self," but this is such a great opportunity to demonstrate that you care for every facet of him or her—mask or no mask. When the masks come off, you get the pleasure of meeting the *real* kid, the survival child.

HOW TO WELCOME WITH SAFETY

When a kid arrives, you might want to start off by laying down rules: "Bedtime's at 9, lights out by 10." It feels like structure, but their trauma reads it as control, sparking fear or rebellion. Rigid rules in the first days will deepen mistrust and invite tests against these new boundaries. Rules without having first established safety tell kids that care is conditional.

Start with safety and comfort: "Want your light on? I'm nearby." I worked with a 9-year-old in an emergency shelter unit, housing him until a foster home became available. Our ritual was that I would read to him every evening at bedtime. Over the weeks, the nighttime ritual led to deep, vulnerable discussions and questions.

One night, as he was going to sleep and I was sitting in his doorway, he said, "Frank, do you know my mom died?"

I replied, "Yeah, I know buddy. I am sorry." We sat in silence for a bit and he eventually said, "I'm glad you are here." Heartbroken, I replied, "Yeah, me too, buddy."

When trust comes, you are going to hear hard things. Trust is the door to calming their survival instincts, leading to a desire to share the burdens of their little hearts in a safe place, a desire to make sense of what's happening to them.

Gather information gently: "What helped at your last place?" Be consistent. Create the same bedtime ritual every night. Repair mistakes: "I rushed you; I'm sorry." Celebrate wins: One choice made is progress. PFA builds trust fast, turning fear into safety.

TOOLS FOR PFA

- **Safety and comfort**: Ask, "Light on or off?" A 7-year-old may be calmed with a nightlight.
- **Offer choices**: Give two options. "Milk or juice?"
- **Playful connection**: Play cards, talk about music or sports. What interests them?
- **Reflect and learn**: Journal: "What scared them? How can I comfort this child?" Example: "He hid food, so I'll offer extra snacks."
- **Build trust**: Commit to one consistent nightly check-in, like "Need anything?"
- **Model repair**: Apologize. "I apologize for rushing you; let's try it again."

HOLDING SPACE FOR YOURSELF

A new kid's fears can overwhelm you. Their tests can quickly spark doubt or frustration. I saw it when an 11-year-old's snack demands triggered her mom's impatience, and her sharp tone hurt the fragile trust she'd worked so hard to build. I helped the two navigate an apology, breathing deeply, and they both stayed steady. Coaching taught me that you can't be their harbor if you're sinking.

You'll stumble, maybe you push rules too soon, or feel drained by their tears. Forgive yourself; you're human. A foster mom felt lost with a 6-year-old's silence. We talked about getting stuck in the *emotion* of the behavior and how we needed to shift to the *why* of the behavior. She journaled, reminding herself she's not supposed to be the savior, only a safe port in the child's current storm.

Who can you talk to about releasing your emotions and getting the support you need? Lean on a local foster group or therapist. Sometimes, hearing the stories of others can encourage us to keep going too. Try mindfulness: five-minute breaths. Your calm is their safety, but you need rest. Don't underestimate the power of good grounding practices when you've been overwhelmed by big emotions: theirs *and* yours. You're building trust, slowly and intentionally.

THE PATH AHEAD

Welcoming a foster kid with your PFA toolkit means meeting their fear with safety rather than rules. Their guardedness is trauma's plea for care. Your steady choices and calm presence rewires their brain, showing trust is real. Progress is slow. Some days, they'll hide or test your patience, and you'll doubt whether you're accomplishing anything in their lives. But remember that you're enough. Each soft question or game plants a seed of security, one that will grow into resilience over time.

You're not just surviving the storm; you're teaching them how to sail through it with you.

Next, in chapter 11, we'll navigate the foster care system's maze, turning frustration into advocacy for the kids you love.

PART 3

Expanding the Anchor– Advocating for Systemic Safety and Lasting Change

CHAPTER 11

Navigating the System– Understanding and Advocating Within Foster Care

The foster care system can feel like a maze with no map. Twisting, often contradictory, rules, overburdened caseworkers, and policies that seem to trap everyone—kids, parents, and workers—can overwhelm the families within the system. I've coached families through the frustration of sudden moves and their ignored pleas for help. I've felt the sting of bureaucracy myself, watching a 13-year-old Indigenous girl slip through the cracks, her rigid guardian's clashes pushing her to the streets, where she felt more in control than at home.

It's easy to point fingers at the worker who missed a visit, the judge who rushed a decision, or the policy that favors quantity over quality. But blame is a dead end. Understanding the system's deep roots in coercion, not connection, helps you find grace for everyone involved and advocate with clear eyes. This chapter shares stories, science, and tools to turn that frustration into focused action, helping you fight for your foster kid without losing your way.

By ninth grade, I was already conditioned to impulsive, risk-taking behavior. When I got to high school, within the first two weeks, I somehow ended up on the roof of the gymnasium in my swim trunks. I remember looking over the edge of the building to see how many feet of concrete I had to clear in order to land in the swimming pool when I jumped. Believe it or not, I made it. I landed in the middle of the pool, scrambled out, and bolted to the locker room.

By then, teachers had called the coach's office. The head football coach came out and there I was: a wet skinny kid. He pointed at me and said, "You! In my office now!" I went into his office, and he asked if I had really jumped off the roof into the pool. I told him yes, and he shook his head with a little chuckle. He thought for a minute and then said, "Well, you have two choices: one, I can call your parents to come get you or, two, I can give you three of these." He then reached behind his filing cabinet and showed me a wooden paddle with holes in it.

I quickly exclaimed, "I will take three of those!" When he was done and I was standing there unable to sit, he again paused. He asked me if I was on the football team. I said no, and he said, "Well, you are now. I'll let the freshman football coach know you are joining."

No rejection. No calling the cops. No relentless emotional abuse at home. Yet, he had a nearly flawless response to the behavior. Dangerous behavior needs consequences, and he offered me a choice. I had some control. He affirmed me by shaking his head in wonder and chuckling a bit. It was a pretty good outcome from my perspective, and I didn't do it again.

I was not a good fit for team sports, though. I had no understanding of sharing or collaboration in that way. That learning would come later. In the end, it was someone who understood kids in a consistent, nonjudgmental way.

The following year brought a new school, new kids, a rural area, and a different culture. Within two weeks of school, I was in a knock-down, drag-out fight with an older kid in class, bleeding and swinging until we were pulled apart, suspended again. When I came back to school, my whole schedule had been changed. I had two periods in the administrator's office, surrounded by five no-nonsense moms who knew how to give me the tough love I needed. My period before lunch was scheduled at the pool, so I swam during that period and many lunches. When it all falls into place, a community solution works best.

WHY THE SYSTEM FEELS BROKEN

The Human Services system, paradoxically, is built on coercion, not connection, and is a legacy of control that echoes from ancient societies guarding resources to modern policies prioritizing quick fixes over healing. Yuval Noah Harari in *Sapiens* traces this back to when humans first farmed abundance, needing armies to protect it, and birthing hierarchies of power over people.[37] Fast forward to today, and it's in the way Families First legislation pushes kinship care

---

37 Yuval Noah Harari, *Sapiens: A Brief History of Humankind* (New York: Harper, 2015), 101.

without enough support, leaving kids in dysfunctional homes that can't provide safety and are supported by young, changing staff who mostly only end up teaching treatment resistance.

Chodura et al. show how underfunded agencies lead to inconsistent care, with foster parents juggling multiple workers who burn out, and pass the chaos to kids.[38] McTavish and McKee highlight foster youth's voices: They feel like pawns in a game of paperwork, moved without warning, their trauma ignored in the rush for "placement."[39]

My work with fostering families nearly always prompts me to remind staff to stop paying so much attention to the details of the behavior. This is the staff's threat detection, which limits their creativity and curiosity. In one case, a young lady was coming into a residential setting after leaving a foster shelter. As the staff problem solved how they were going to receive her, I was going through her paperwork and what jumped out at me was how many transitions she had endured in the last two years…thirty times! She had moved thirty times!

I stopped the meeting, gave this detail to the staff, and asked them, "What is she good at?" "Arriving and leaving" were the answers, along with controlling when she leaves by making it unbearable for those taking care of her. We then looked at her trauma history, and it became clear that her history would be

---

38 S. Chodura, S. Lohrmann, and S. Sommer, "Foster Parents' Parenting and the Social-Emotional Development and Adaptive Functioning of Children in Foster Care: A PRISMA-Guided Literature Review and Meta-Analysis," *Clinical Child and Family Psychology Review* 24, no. 2 (2021): 326–47, https://doi.org/10.1007/s10567-021-00349-y.

39 J. R. McTavish and C. McKee, "Foster Children's Perspectives on Participation in Child Welfare Processes: A Meta-Synthesis of Qualitative Studies," *PLoS One* 17, no. 10 (2022): e0275784, https://doi.org/10.1371/journal.pone.0275784.

more useful for designing the way we would receive her. In this instance, we actually had the paperwork. Many foster parents know that often the child comes without paperwork, history, or even a narrative of what happened to them. While HIPAA is meant to protect the client, it often produces more chaos and damage than necessary and should be reevaluated to protect our foster parent community.

WHAT SYSTEMIC CHALLENGES LOOK LIKE

Systemic challenges show up as a 10-year-old boy, moved three times in a year, acting out in school due to the instability. His outbursts were a cry for someone to notice the chaos and his expectation of being moved suddenly without warning. His internal response was to control when the move occurred by acting out violent behavior, triggering a move on his timeline rather than waiting for someone else to move him unexpectedly.

Or a 16-year-old girl who was denied therapy due to budget cuts, her anger growing as workers rotated in and out of her life. She finally ended up in the juvenile justice system because of her frustration and rage against the system.

While trying to come to mediation between a rigid caregiver and a 13-year-old girl, Families First pushed a kinship placement. But without support, the guardian didn't know how to handle her deep emotions and she ran away at 13, lost to the streets.

These aren't isolated incidents. They're the system's echoes where understaffed workers miss visits, policies favor speed over healing, and kids pay the price.

QTIP: Quit Taking It Personally.

Their frustration isn't yours to carry; it's the system's weight on their shoulders.

HOW TO NAVIGATE AND ADVOCATE

What Doesn't Work

When the system stalls, you might lash out at caseworkers or withdraw, feeling defeated. It's human to want to fight or flee, but it backfires. Many caseworkers and social workers are in various stages of compassion fatigue, struggling with the effects of vicarious and secondary trauma themselves. Still, others hold on to the mentalist model of behavior and don't believe in trauma-informed practices. Lashing out or giving up drains you, isolates your kid, and reinforces the system's flaws. It's a no-go zone that keeps everyone stuck.

What Does Work

Seeing the system as a shared struggle. Caseworkers are overwhelmed too. Many have such a large caseload that all they can do is put out fires. How we got here is a whole book in itself that needs to be written.

Start with curiosity: "What's blocking her therapy?" I worked with a mom of a 10-year-old; she calmly asked about play therapy options, securing it after weeks of gentle persistence.

Learn policies like Families First, which funds prevention. Use it to request training or resources. Join foster groups for support and encouragement. Persistence can shift systems. When you advocate for PFA, Rainbowdance, SPR, or ARC, you're turning barriers into bridges. The NCTSN website gives you a valid place to start.

TOOLS FOR NAVIGATING THE SYSTEM

- **Ask questions**: "What services fit her needs?"
- **Learn policies**: Ask the case workers questions. Read Families First guidelines online.
- **Join groups**: Connect with foster networks for resources.
- **Reflect and learn**: Journal: "What's the barrier? How can I help my child heal?"
- **Build trust**: Meet workers calmly: "Let's help him together."

HOLDING SPACE FOR YOURSELF

Systemic barriers, like frequent moves and budget cuts, can feel like gut punches, sparking anger or despair. Over the years, **QTIP** has saved my emotional battery, letting me check myself and return to critical thinking. Coaching taught me: You can't advocate if you're burned out. To gain a deeper understanding of systemic issues, Dr. Sandra Bloom's books *Creating Sanctuary*, *Destroying Sanctuary*, and *Restoring Sanctuary* are important reads.

THE PATH AHEAD

Navigating foster care means seeing its flaws—coercion, inconsistency—and advocating with grace. Kids' frustration is the system's responsibility, not yours. Your persistence, questions, and calm push for change and rewire their trust in care. Progress is slow—some days, workers stall, and you'll doubt. You're enough. Each call or meeting builds stability.

Next, in chapter 12, we'll explore saying good goodbyes—preparing kids for transitions with rituals. We'll share stories and tools to foster independence, helping kids carry trust forward into their future.

CHAPTER 12

Saying Good Goodbyes- Preparing Kids for Transition

Saying goodbye to a foster kid, whether they're aging out or moving to a new home, feels like letting go of a piece of your heart. Their trauma makes transitions terrifying, but your rituals can ground them, giving them trust to carry forward. I've coached teens leaving care who were lost to the streets without connection and learned that rituals like photos or hugs build lasting bridges. This chapter shares stories, science, and tools to prepare kids for independence or new homes, turning goodbyes into hope.

MY STORY: A LASTING CONNECTION

While getting my clinical master's degree, I had the great fortune to work with a very skilled team in the Midwest as part of my consulting and training contract. I was working with a young person who was institutionalized. Her ability to get under staff's skin was a constant irritation for most of them. Because of the way I worked under a supervisor while doing therapy with her, the girl viewed me differently, more as a student like her than as an authority figure. We connected over the ten sessions I did with her, and she taught me a lot.

As I neared the end of my practicum, I knew I had to develop a healthy way to say goodbye. I needed a good transition ritual. I thought about it and made a plan. So when we met for one of our final sessions together, I informed her that I would no longer see her in this capacity. However, all my great transition ideas disappeared in an instant when she quickly interrupted me and told me to get out of her therapy session (her main therapist was in the room supervising me). She said I was wasting her time. Using several expletives, she let me know her opinion. As I backed out the door, I assured her I would still be around, just not in this capacity. She told me that she was done with me.

I was surprised by her instant, vehement response; however, I had already been trained to understand the root causes of her reaction. Because of my own experiences with loss and transition, I did not take it personally. Her perception was what mattered and holding space for her emotions was the correct response. It also came from a deep place of knowing what it is like to feel rejected and to have someone leave you again.

I continued to see her in the hallways and at mealtimes while doing coaching and consultation. She would either ignore me or call me a traitor as we passed each other in the hallway.

Over time, as this agency did its wonderful work, she transitioned to a step-down unit in a different city, preparing for foster care and adoption. A few weeks later, I was working in that program, and I asked about her. The staff told me where she was in the building, so I made my way toward her living space. As I walked down the hallway, she emerged from her room. When she saw me, she instantly screamed my name and ran toward me. She hugged me with all her might, crying, and of course I was crying too.

The point is that even when they reject you, stay constant. **QTIP.** They are fiercely defending their vulnerability. It's not about you. In our final therapy session, she needed to reject me before I could reject her. Remember: This is about the deep perceptions within her own mind, not that I was actually rejecting her. But when she saw me in a new setting, her instinctive sense that I was safe and approachable won over her fears of abandonment. She had made a lot of progress between those two interactions with me. Now her brain knew it was safe to race toward me. Subconsciously, she knew she would find unconditional regard and safety.

The world of foster care is vastly different now than it was before 2016. Families First legislation changed the landscape in dramatic ways for foster care across the country. A large number of for-profit adolescent treatment centers have emerged for kids in the West. For-profit inevitably means cherry-picking kids. The most tortured children will continue to be rejected, even though they need a soft place to land the most.

Foster care has moved from institutions into homes. Young, inexperienced, and under trained staff are asked to go into homes and make a difference without fully understanding the dynamics they are working with. While well-meaning, it is not working out in execution. Underfunded, under resourced, and overwhelmed, foster care staff across the country are resorting to babysitting kids in hotels and in their offices because there are too many kids and not enough home placements available.

We have to understand what kids are actually experiencing. Looking at a behavior without intellectual curiosity is professionally lazy and unproductive. To understand the depth of how much we need to shift our perspective, foster and adoptive care agencies should commit to reading chapters 5 and 6 of *Trauma and Recovery* by Dr. Judith Herman. Those two chapters should set the tone for a new vision and practice in foster care work and the training of adoptive parents and staff. We need to commit to building a continuum of care focused on quality of life for all those kids and those who work in the field of child abuse and recovery. A continuum of care means a spectrum of services—from immediate safety (like PFA in the first days) to long-term healing (like EMDR or TF-CBT)—tailored to a kid's needs as they move through trauma's stages. It's not a one-size-fits-all fix; it's a ladder they climb step by step, with supports at every rung.

We know what to do; it's been measured in programs like Voices in Sonoma, CA, where aftercare for aging-out youth reduced homelessness by 40% through consistent mentoring.[40] This proof shows that when we connect kids to ongoing care, they don't just survive—they thrive. As foster parents, you're the first rung advocate for that continuum, from your home to the next placement, ensuring no kid falls through the cracks.

---

40 Families Rising, *Relationships and Sexuality: How to Support Youth in Foster Care and Adoption* (Families Rising, 2024), 23.

Of course, not every kid in foster care is traumatized to the same degree, but all are experiencing toxic stress, which continues to activate a brain built on fear and anger. The tools I am suggesting here will work equally well for all kids who struggle.

WHY TRANSITIONS ARE HARD

Trauma makes foster kids fear abandonment in transitions. Steenbakkers et al. found foster youth crave belonging, yet expect rejection, making goodbyes feel final.[41] Purvis et al. note that their brain, wired for loss, struggles with change unless anchored by rituals.[42] My work with Voices in Sonoma showed that 18-year-olds flamed out in college without emotional grounding. Free state tuition didn't replace the need for stable, consistent connection.

HOW TO PREPARE FOR TRANSITIONS

When a kid is leaving, you might rush goodbyes or avoid them, fearing pain. It feels easier, but it leaves kids feeling unmoored. Avoiding or rushing goodbyes deepens their fear of loss.

Build rituals early. It can be something as simple as taking a joyful photo while playing cards or laughing, then hanging it up with other family photos in your living room. This says "You're part of us." Develop ways to communicate to the child

---

41 Annemiek Steenbakkers et al., "Foster Children's Views of Family: A Systematic Review and Qualitative Synthesis," *Children and Youth Services Review* 121 (2021): Article 105879, https://doi.org/10.1016/j.childyouth.2020.105879.

42 Karyn B. Purvis, David R. Cross, and Wendy L. Sunshine, *The Connected Child: Bring Hope and Healing to Your Adoptive Family*, updated ed. (New York: McGraw-Hill, 2019), 89–91.

that even when they are away you are thinking about them. A certain song, TV show, or activity reminds you of them and can promote long-term connection and grounding even after they are gone. In some school districts, we use summer postcards. The teachers and counselors send out monthly postcards of good thoughts and encouraging statements that let the child know that someone is thinking of them.

TOOLS FOR GOOD GOODBYES

- **Photo rituals**: Take a joy-filled photo and hang it. "You belong."
- **Gesture rituals**: Create a handshake or wave just between the two of you.
- **Teach practical skills**: Practice budgeting or job talks.
- **Reflect and learn**: Journal: "What scares them about leaving? How can I help them navigate this next challenge?"
- **Build trust**: Commit to one ritual, like a weekly game, early on.

HOLDING SPACE FOR YOURSELF

Goodbyes in foster care cut deep, like a wave pulling you under just when you thought you'd caught your breath. Watching a kid pack their bag or wave from the car, their face a mix of hope and fear, can stir a grief that sneaks up on you. It brings guilt for the moments you weren't perfect, sorrow for the time you had, or a hollow ache wondering if you gave them enough. It's the quiet after the door closes that hits hardest, leaving you to sift through the what-ifs.

I've felt that pull, saying goodbye to a 16-year-old boy I'd coached through his rages and doubts. He hugged me tight, whispering, "Thank you," before heading off to his new home. I stood there, chest tight, replaying our every interaction, until I realized: My stumbles didn't erase the bridges we built. That's the truth for you too. Goodbyes don't measure your worth; they honor the love you poured in.

You'll wrestle with that grief, maybe avoiding the last hug or replaying "if onlys" late at night. It's okay to let it wash over you; you're a human carrying not just your heart, but also their heart. Don't let it drown you. Honor the goodbye with your own ritual. Write a letter to the kid, tucking it away as a reminder of the light you sparked, or light a candle for the family they're joining, sending silent wishes for their health and safety.

These acts aren't about erasing the hurt; they're about transforming it into a quiet strength, a way to hold space for the joy they brought and the growth you shared. Lean into what grounds you: a walk where you let the wind carry your what-ifs away, or a call to a fellow foster parent who gets the ache without words.

This grief is part of the beauty, proof you loved fiercely. It doesn't mean you failed; it means you showed up, steady and real, in a world that often isn't. Celebrate the echoes, like a kid who waves back or a call from their new home. You're not just letting go; you're launching them with the anchor of your love, a piece of safety they'll carry forever. You're enough for that release, and for the next hello.

Keep loving, keep holding space. For them, for you, for the families who come after. Your heart is the ripple that changes everything.

THE PATH AHEAD

Good goodbyes give foster kids rituals to carry trust forward. Their fear is trauma's echo, not rejection. Your photos, hugs, and skills rewire their brains for resilience. Progress is slow. Some days, they'll pull away, and you'll feel as if your heart is being pulled out of your chest. You are enough. Each ritual builds a bridge toward safety and resilience that the child will carry with them wherever they go.

Finally, as we round out this book, in chapter 13, we'll share a toolkit of trauma-informed resources like ARC, Rainbowdance, and more.

CHAPTER 13

Your Toolkit–Resources for Trauma-Informed Care

Foster parenting children with traumatic backgrounds is a journey of patience, resilience, and heart. This toolkit offers a guiding formula to create healing environments, grounded in trust and understanding. By keeping these principles at the forefront, you'll reduce burnout, avoid secondary trauma, and foster hope for the kids in your care. Each tool is designed to meet children where they are, honoring their lived experiences while gently guiding them toward safety and connection.

1. SAFETY FIRST

Safety forms the foundation for any real healing in foster care. In essence, it's the state where someone feels shielded from harm, peril, or unexpected threats. For foster kids, this goes beyond physical protection—it's about that inner sense of security in their surroundings, even when there's no obvious danger lurking. Start by carving out peaceful nooks in your home, like a soft corner piled with pillows or a quiet area for simple games like Jenga. Your consistent, grounded presence acts as a quiet signal, gently nudging their brain from constant survival mode toward a place of genuine trust.

2. ONE THING AT A TIME

Building relationships is the foundation for trust, and it happens slowly, one moment at a time. A single game of checkers or a shared laugh can plant a seed for connection. Rushing or expecting quick fixes can overwhelm a child already burdened by trauma. Focus on small, intentional interactions to show the child they're seen and valued.

3. YOU ARE NOT A SAVIOR

This work isn't about you as the hero. It's about empowering the child to find their own strength. Let go of the need to "fix" them—it can cloud your ability to listen and respond to their needs. Your role is to guide, not rescue, ensuring the child's journey remains their own.

4. QUIT TAKING IT PERSONALLY (QTIP)

When a child lashes out or shuts down, it's not about you. It's their fear speaking. Their chaos, born of trauma, can feel personal, but it's a survival reflex. Pause, breathe, and remind yourself that their reactions stem from pain, not rejection. This mindset keeps you grounded and open to the child's needs.

5. CONSISTENCY

Children from traumatic backgrounds often cling to chaos, craving control in a world that feels unpredictable. Your consistency, steady routines, and calm responses counter this. Even after disruptions, return to predictable patterns as soon as you can. A consistent dinner time or bedtime ritual can become an anchor, showing the child that stability is possible.

6. PREDICTABILITY

Once consistency is established, a predictable environment works like a balm for a child's nervous system. Knowing what to expect, when meals happen, and how you'll respond creates a calming effect. For example, a daily schedule or a familiar greeting each morning can ease their anxiety, helping them feel secure.

7. UNCONDITIONAL REGARD

A child's chaos will test your ability to care without judgment, but unconditional regard is nonnegotiable. Their outbursts or withdrawals can feel like rejection, so you must actively recommit to seeing their worth. This might mean taking a moment to journal or breathe deeply to re-center yourself. Your unwavering care shows the child they're valued, no matter their behavior.

8. VALIDATE THEIR PERCEPTION

Every child's worldview is shaped by their life experiences, often filled with betrayal or loss. Validate their perspective without necessarily agreeing or excusing their behavior. For example, if a child believes adults can't be trusted, acknowledge their reality: "It makes sense you feel that way after what you've been through." This builds trust, but only works once safety and consistency are in place. From there, you can gently introduce new ways of seeing the world, showing the child that not all adults will disappoint them.

9. ELIMINATE "IF" AND "BUT"

Phrases like "If you had listened, this wouldn't have happened" or "But you should've known better" shift blame and demand conditional obedience, which children with trauma can't process. Instead, focus on age-appropriate connections between actions and outcomes. A 10-year-old might hear, "I see you're upset. Let's figure out what happened and how we can make it better." This avoids blame and honors their history, fostering accountability without shame.

10. UNDERSTAND TEMPERAMENT

Every child's temperament shapes the way they experience the world. Highly sensitive children, common among those with trauma, need extra reassurance and connection. A loud classroom might overwhelm one child, but not another. Notice their cues. Does a raised voice make them flinch? Offer tailored support, like a quiet break or a gentle check-in, to meet their unique needs. Understanding temperament is vital. If you have a temperament that is stress resistant, then it will be harder for you to understand what someone who is sensitive is going through. Being sensitive is not a bad thing. It is a necessary character trait that contributes to a balanced community. Just look at some of the people you most revere—musicians, poets, philosophers, actors, activists. Sensitive people who are supported as needed contribute to society and safe communities in ways that are vital for our community's health.

WHY THIS MATTERS

These tools aren't just strategies. They're a lifeline. By prioritizing safety, trust, and understanding, you reduce the risk of burnout and secondary trauma for yourself while creating space for healing in the children you care for. Your steady presence, guided by these principles, shows kids they're worth staying for, worth loving. Keep these tools close, and you'll build a path of hope, one small moment at a time.

ARMING YOURSELF TO HEAL

Foster parenting is a journey through rough waters, but the right tools can steady your course. I've coached families and seen how evidence-based interventions, like ARC or Rainbowdance, turn chaos into connection. This chapter isn't a dry list; it's a conversation, like sitting with a friend, sharing proven resources to help you advocate for your foster child. These tools, grounded in science, fit children of all ages and needs, empowering you to heal and build trust.

HOW TO USE AND ADVOCATE FOR RESOURCES

When a kid struggles, you might stick to generic parenting books or wait for caseworkers to offer help. It feels safe, but it misses out on the true depths of trauma's effects. Explore evidence-based tools below and advocate for your kid. Many training sessions are free online. Share resources in your foster groups. Advocacy gets tools to kids who need it most. Build bridges of safety, trust, and consistency.

YOUR TRAUMA-INFORMED TOOLKIT

- **ARC Model (Attachment, Regulation, Competency):** Builds trust and self-regulation through play and connection. Uses games like Jenga to teach boundaries.
- **Rainbowdance:** Uses music and movement to regulate emotions. Kids follow a leader's moves, building trust. Find trainers at ChildTrauma.org.
- **EMDR (Eye Movement Desensitization and Reprocessing):** For ages 6 and over, processes trauma through guided eye movements or other bilateral stimulation.
- **TF-CBT (Trauma-Focused Cognitive Behavioral Therapy):** For ages 6 and over, it is an evidence-based treatment approach designed to help children and adolescents who have experienced traumatic events, such as sexual abuse, physical abuse, or natural disasters.
- **TANT (Trauma Art Narrative Therapy):** Structured, cognitive exposure technique that combines art, written word, and storytelling to help individuals process traumatic events and reduce distressing symptoms like flashbacks and nightmares. The process involves creating sequential drawings of the trauma, which helps to integrate fragmented memories, and then using these drawings to build a cohesive narrative in a supportive, non-interpretive environment. No artistic ability is needed. TANT gives individuals a way to feel seen and

to partner with their therapist to heal from shame, guilt, and fear associated with the trauma.

- **Sanctuary Model**: Creates trauma-informed communities in homes and schools. It emphasizes safety and shared goals. Find training at TheSanctuaryInstitute. org.

HOLDING SPACE FOR YOURSELF

Searching for resources can feel like chasing shadows— frustrating when tools aren't available or workers dismiss you. Researching the NCTSN site will give you fact sheets, training, and tools to advocate for resources from a position of proven validity. You can also find local or regional sites that are actively engaged in NCTSN training or tool development.

Conditioning yourself to use this site can calm your frustration, help you feel understood, and support you as you learn new tools and resources to help your child.

THE PATH AHEAD

This toolkit isn't just a list—it's your compass for the road ahead, equipping you with proven resources like ARC, Rainbowdance, and EMDR to cut through trauma's fog and light the way for your foster kid. Their pain isn't a mark against you; it's an invitation to advocate and stand in the gap between what the system offers and what your child truly needs. When you push for those tools, you're not just accessing help. You're showing them, in the clearest way, that they're worth the fight. Your voice in a meeting, your persistence with a caseworker saying, "Let's try Rainbowdance for her meltdowns," isn't a battle cry; it's a quiet revolution, rewiring not only their brain for trust but the world around them for compassion.

Progress won't be a straight line. Some days, the system stonewalls you, resources feel out of reach, and doubts creep in like shadows at dusk. Did my efforts help? Is this enough? You're creating ripples of trust—one steady act at a time—turning scarcity into abundance, fear into fortitude. You're enough. Your heart, your persistence, and your willingness to show up messy and real makes a difference. Forgive the stumbles, the nights you replay the "what ifs," and lean into the small victories such as a kid who waves goodbye without flinching or a teacher who nods in understanding at your ARC suggestion. These moments are the beacons proving your love is landing on fertile ground.

This book ends here, but your story does not. Carry these tools into your home, your school meetings, and your quiet moments of doubt. Keep loving anyway, advocating fiercely, and showing up with that unconditional regard for them and for you. You're not just a foster parent—you're a builder of futures, one safe harbor at a time. And in that, you're already changing the world.

Your Love Is Their Anchor

You've journeyed far through these pages, peering into the hidden storms of trauma that wire foster kids for survival, running from fear, fighting for control, or freezing in shame. And you are discovering how your steady, loving presence can be the calm that guides them home.

From the raw ache of a new arrival's silence to the fierce advocacy needed in schools and systems, you've seen that fostering isn't about fixing broken kids. It's about meeting them in their chaos with open arms and an open heart. As Maya Angelou so wisely said, "When we knew better, we did better." You're doing better every day, and because of that you're already their hero.

Don't chase perfection—it's a trap that leaves you exhausted and doubting. Whether it's a 7-year-old clinging to a teddy bear like it's their last lifeline or a 16-year-old testing your limits with slammed doors and sharp words, your response matters. Your soft voice in the quiet aftermath, the patient game of Jenga where you laugh off a toppled tower, or the simple "I'm here, and I see you" whispered during a meltdown—these are the moments that rewrite their story. They show a kid who's only known conditional love that they're worthy just as they are, strings and all.

Remember, that same grace is for you. Forgive the days when frustration boils over or doubt creeps in and the tired evenings when you wonder if you're making a difference. You are. Small, consistent acts—a deep breath before responding, a journal entry to untangle your worries, or leaning on a foster group for a laugh and a vent—reshape trauma's chaos not just for them, but for you too. Your care is a two-way street. As you nurture their healing, you heal your own heart. Take that breath, go for a walk, or call a friend. Recharge because your light is what they need to find their way.

This work doesn't stop at your front door; it ripples out, touching schools, agencies, and communities that so often fail our kids. Imagine how our foster kids could be transformed in a world where every teacher knows ARC, every caseworker practices PFA, and foster groups share Rainbowdance rituals like old friends passing a favorite recipe.

You're the one who can start that wave by advocating for trauma-informed training in your district, sharing a goodbye photo ritual with a new foster parent, or pushing back against the cradle-to-prison pipeline by speaking up for a kid's needs. That's the power of your imperfect love. It doesn't just hold one child; it lights the path for generations. Keep showing up, keep loving fiercely, keep remembering: You're enough, and so are they. Your heart is their anchor, and together, you'll weather any storm.

Connect With Frank to Build a Trauma-Informed Future

You've walked through the storms of foster parenting—kids running, fighting, or freezing, systems that are frustrating, and moments when you doubted yourself. I've been there, messing up when I pushed a kid too hard, and I learned that love—not control—builds trust. Now, you're ready to turn the lessons in these pages into action, creating a safe harbor for your kids and your community. I'm Frank Grijalva, and I'm here to guide you with the same raw heart and hard-won lessons that filled this book. Let's keep building futures where every foster kid feels seen, safe, and enough.

Imagine your home or agency transformed: play calming kids, schools embracing ARC, communities catching kids before they fall. I offer **speaking engagements** that spark hope, sharing stories to inspire foster parents and workers.

My **jump-start trainings** shift agency cultures by teaching trauma-informed tools like PFA and Rainbowdance to replace control with connection, as I did with Voices in Sonoma. For deeper change, my **long-term consultations** partner with you or your agency to embed strategies like ARC, tailoring plans to your kids' needs. And yes, I'll toss in a dolphin story or two—because joy heals too!

Ready to start? Download my free "Trauma-Informed Starter Kit" at SocialCapitalLogistics.com. It's packed with PFA scripts and play rituals to try tonight. Book me for a talk, training, or consultation by emailing frank@SocialCapitalLogistics.com.

As Maya Angelou said, "When we knew better, we did better." Let's do better together—your love is the anchor kids need.

ABOUT THE AUTHOR

Frank Grijalva is the Director of Midwest Trauma Services Network and the Senior Vice President of Programming for The International Trauma Center. He works with various state and local agencies across the country ranging from tribal child welfare, disability services culture change, juvenile justice facility consultation, and school districts. Frank works at the regional and local systems level, as well as individual case consultations for agencies.

Frank came through the California system as a child, adopted into a family challenged by mental health and substance abuse issues. Raised in the East Bay Area of Northern California, Frank attended nine different schools in his first nine years. Growing up in a difficult home in a challenging environment both geographically and historically, Frank has a unique perspective that translates for many of our most traumatized communities, families, and children.

Frank found his way into the military. His first professional training was as a special warfare diver attached to the United States Navy's Marine Mammal Program. He spent eight years honing behavior modification skills, stress management, and understanding the dynamics of nonverbal communication.

Later, as a stay-at-home dad for two kids and a student of psychology, he became aware of and struggled with development, his own trauma exposure, and behavioral progressions and sequencing. At 40, Frank was diagnosed with childhood PTSD. This led to a journey of self-exploration and an academic focus on psychological trauma.

Frank has worked with the International Trauma Center since 1999 and deployed to Ground Zero to manage a team of clinicians working with a federal agency in "the dig" to support them ongoing as they did their difficult work. Frank also worked extensively throughout Louisiana and Mississippi in the aftermath of Katrina. Additionally, Frank has worked abroad in Israel, Gaza and the West Bank, Nepal, Jordan, Haiti, and several other countries for agencies like Save the Children, USAID, the World Bank, and the International Center for the Protection of Victims of Torture, developing interventions and trained by a variety of world class clinicians working with children.

As Director of the Midwest Trauma Services Network and Senior Vice President of Programming for the International Trauma Center, he has spent the last several years introducing and training selected trauma informed evidence-based practices, as well as designing and implementing innovations specific to people from at-risk environments through the Office of Juvenile Justice and Delinquency Prevention in the US federal government. Frank has a BS in Disaster Psychology with an emphasis on mental health, an MS in Public Health with a focus on child mental health, and an MS in Clinical Counseling with trauma theory as the primary theoretical framework. Frank is the proud father of two gifted and resilient children who contribute in significant ways in their chosen professions. His mission is to create a world that understands the impact of trauma and abuse on children, families, communities, and culture by teaching, challenging, and learning everywhere he goes.

BIBLIOGRAPHY

Blaustein, Margaret E., and Kristine M. Kinniburgh. *Treating Traumatic Stress in Children and Adolescents.* 2nd ed. Guilford Press, 2018.

Chodura, Sonja, Susanne Lohrmann, and Sarah Sommer. "Foster Parents' Parenting and the Social-Emotional Development and Adaptive Functioning of Children in Foster Care: A PRISMA-Guided Literature Review and Meta-analysis." *Clinical Child and Family Psychology Review* 24, no. 2 (2021): 326–47.

Cohen, Judith A., Anthony P. Mannarino, and Esther Deblinger. *Treating Trauma and Traumatic Grief in Children and Adolescents.* 2nd ed. Guilford Press, 2017.

Engler, Amy D., Kofi O. Sarpong, Barbara S. Van Horne, Cynthia S. Greeley, and Richard S. Keefe. "A Systematic Review of Mental Health Disorders of Children in Foster Care." *Trauma, Violence, & Abuse* 23, no. 1 (2022): 255–64.

Families Rising. *Relationships and Sexuality: How to Support Youth in Foster Care and Adoption.* Families Rising, 2024.

Felitti, Vincent J., Robert F. Anda, Dale Nordenberg, David F. Williamson, Alison M. Spitz, Valerie Edwards, Mary P. Koss, and James S. Marks. "Relationship of Childhood Abuse and Household Dysfunction to Many of the Leading Causes of Death in Adults: The Adverse Childhood Experiences (ACE) Study." *American Journal of Preventive Medicine* 14, no. 4 (1998): 245–58.

Gussak, David. *Art and Art Therapy with the Imprisoned.* Routledge, 2019.

Harari, Yuval Noah. *Sapiens: A Brief History of Humankind.* Harper, 2015.

Herman, Judith L. *Trauma and Recovery: The Aftermath of Violence—From Domestic Abuse to Political Terror.* Updated ed. Basic Books, 2022.

Kahneman, Daniel. *Thinking, Fast and Slow.* Farrar, Straus and Giroux, 2011.

Knotts Family Agency. *How Do You Discipline a Foster Child?* Knotts Family Agency, 2021. https://knottsfamilyagency.org/how-do-you-discipline-a-foster-child/.

McTavish, Jill R., and Catherine McKee. "Foster Children's Perspectives on Participation in Child Welfare Processes: A Meta-synthesis of Qualitative Studies." *PLoS One* 17, no. 10 (2022): e0275784. https://doi.org/10.1371/journal.pone.0275784.

Mischel, Walter, Ebbe B. Ebbesen, and Antonette R. Zeiss. "Cognitive and Attentional Mechanisms in Delay of Gratification." *Journal of Personality and Social Psychology* 21, no. 2 (1972): 204–18. https://doi.org/10.1037/h0032198.

National Child Traumatic Stress Network (NCTSN). *Child Trauma Toolkit for Educators.* NCTSN, 2018. https://www.nctsn.org/resources/child-trauma-toolkit-educators.

Pemberton, Sarah, and William Wheeler. *Trauma-Informed Parenting for Foster and Adoptive Families.* Independently published, 2023.

Perry, Bruce D., and Maia Szalavitz. *The Boy Who Was Raised as a Dog: And Other Stories from a Child Psychiatrist's Notebook—What Traumatized Children Can Teach Us about Loss, Love, and Healing.* Basic Books, 2006.

Purvis, Karyn B., David R. Cross, and Wendy L. Sunshine. *The Connected Child: Bring Hope and Healing to Your Adoptive Family*. Updated ed. McGraw-Hill, 2019.

SAMHSA. *Psychological First Aid for Schools Field Operations Guide*. Substance Abuse and Mental Health Services Administration, 2020. https://www.samhsa.gov/resource/dbhis/psychological-first-aid-schools-pfa-s-field-operations-guide-2nd-edition

Shapiro, Francine. *Eye Movement Desensitization and Reprocessing (EMDR) Therapy*. 3rd ed. Guilford Press, 2018.

Siegel, Daniel J. *The Developing Mind: How Relationships and the Brain Interact to Shape Who We Are*. 2nd ed. Guilford Press, 2012.

Steenbakkers, Anne, Ingrid T. Ellingsen, Susan van der Steen, and Hans Grietens. "Foster Children's Views of Family: A Systematic Review and Qualitative Synthesis." *Children and Youth Services Review* 121 (2021): 105879. https://doi.org/10.1016/j.childyouth.2020.105879.

The Education Hub. *Putting Relationships Centre-stage: Strategies for Developing Positive Relationships with Children*. The Education Hub, 2020. https://theeducationhub.org.nz/putting-relationships-centre-stage/.

van der Kolk, Bessel A. *The Body Keeps the Score: Brain, Mind, and Body in the Healing of Trauma*. Viking, 2014.

APPENDIX
Resources and Recommendations

This appendix is your quick-reference guide to trauma-informed tools and resources mentioned throughout the book. It's a starting point for you, the foster parent, to advocate for your kid and build a supportive network. Each entry includes a brief description, why it matters, and how to get started. Reach out to me at MidwestTrauma.org or NCTSN for trainings; many are free or low-cost. Remember, you don't need to be an expert—just a curious guide.

Psychological First Aid (PFA) for Schools

- **Description**: A framework for supporting kids after stress or trauma, with steps like ensuring safety, offering comfort, and gathering information without pressure.
- **Why It Matters**: Helps new arrivals or meltdown moments by focusing on immediate needs, reducing fear and building trust fast.
- **How to Start**: Download the free guide at Store.Samhsa. gov. Practice with a child: "Want your light on?" Train via NCTSN webinars.

ARC Model (Attachment, Regulation, Competency)

- **Description**: Blaustein and Kinniburgh (2018) model for trauma recovery, focusing on secure relationships (attachment), calming emotions (regulation), and building skills (competency).
- **Why It Matters**: Tailors support to kids' trauma, helping in schools or homes to shift from chaos to calm.
- **How to Start**: Request ARC training from NCTSN or local agencies. Example: Daily check-ins for attachment, breathing for regulation.

Rainbowdance™

- **Description**: A movement-based program using music, rhythm, and play to regulate emotions and build connection.
- **Why It Matters**: Turns hypervigilance into joy, teaching self-regulation through fun for ages 4 to 12.
- **How to Start**: Find trainers at childtrauma.org or NCTSN. Try at home: Follow a song's beat together.
- https://www.Bostoncf.org/rainbowdance/

EMDR (Eye Movement Desensitization and Reprocessing)

- **Description**: Therapy using guided eye movements to process trauma memories, reducing flashbacks and fear.
- **Why It Matters**: Helps older kids (6+) release stuck trauma, improving focus and emotions.
- **How to Start**: Ask therapists for EMDR certification. Free NCTSN guides at nctsn.org.

TF-CBT (Trauma-Focused Cognitive Behavioral Therapy)

- **Description**: This model combines talk and play to address trauma for ages 6 to 18, reducing symptoms like nightmares.
- **Why It Matters**: Builds coping skills, turning fear into confidence.
- **How to Start**: Check agency offerings or NCTSN for providers. Home version: share a "worry box" for drawings.

TANT (Trauma Art Narrative Therapy)

- **Description**: Art and storytelling-based therapy to process trauma, no artistic skill needed.
- **Why It Matters**: Helps kids express pain without words, fostering healing for ages 6–18.
- **How to Start**: NCTSN resources at nctsn.org. At home: draw a "trauma story" sequence.

Sanctuary Model

- **Description**: A community-wide approach to trauma-informed care, emphasizing safety and shared goals (thesanctuaryinstitute.org).
- **Why It Matters**: Transforms homes or schools into healing environments for all ages.
- **How to Start**: Free intro training online at TheSanctuaryInstitute.org.

Child and Adolescent Trauma Recovery Intervention (CBI)

- **Description**: CBI is a 5- or 10-week (10-session) group program, using structured play, learning, and creative problem-solving activities to process trauma.
- **Why It Matters**: Turns overwhelming emotions into safe expression through play, boosting safety, self-control, and peer/adult relationships without shame.
- **How to Start**: Contact The Children's Trauma Recovery Foundation at childtraumafoundation.org or NCTSN (nctsn.org) for local facilitators.

Additional Recommendations

- **NCTSN Resources**: Free fact sheets, toolkits, and trainings on trauma-informed care at nctsn.org. Start with the Child Trauma Toolkit for Educators.
- **Families Rising**: Support for foster and adoptive families, including guides on relationships at FamiliesRising.org.
- **Midwest Trauma Services Network (MTSN)**: Frank's network for trainings in PFA, SPR, and PTSM at MidwestTrauma.org.
- **International Trauma Center (ITC)**: Global resources for trauma interventions at InternationalTraumaCenter.com.

Use these resources to advocate: email a teacher an NCTSN fact sheet or request ARC training. You're not alone; these resources are your allies in building trust and healing.

www.ingramcontent.com/pod-product-compliance
Lightning Source LLC
Chambersburg PA
CBHW051803050726
47598CB00006B/2399